To: SANDI

GOD SAID TO ABRAHAM — "TRUST
AND OBEY ME... AND YOUR Descendants
will be more than the SAND in THE
Sea"

Acknowledgements

Whenever we start and finish a project successfully, there is usually an overwhelming sense of relief and satisfaction. But we should never forget that our achievements, are never entirely our own, and they are never accomplished without the support of many others.

I wish to acknowledge my good friend and colleague Dr. Hugh (Solo) Holder M.D. who himself is a facilitator of meaningful change. His vision of what our role in life should be motivated me to search deep inside of me to produce this book, after I saw the type of changes he himself was making in medicine and for others.

I wish to acknowledge the American College of Physician Executives (A.C.P.E) for the brilliant program that they produce to inspire physicians to become leaders. The A.C.P.E provided me with the tools I needed to use in sharpening and honing skills that I already possessed but never recognized that I had. I especially wish to acknowledge Lee Kaiser PhD for removing the blinders from my eyes and helping me to see the world again with the same broadened vision that I originally had when I first decided on a medical career.

To Eric Berkowitz PhD, Hugh Long PhD, Leonard Marcus PhD and Roger Schenke M.D. you are the very best in your respective fields and I hope that the knowledge that I gained from you will assist me to continue to produce more books that will motivate and inspire others to achieve their own dreams as I have done with mine.

To all those individuals, patients, friends and colleagues who encouraged me in any way possible, your words of encouragement helped to keep me going and I thank you sincerely. You know who you are but if you don't know who you are, you can call me and I will thank you personally. I specifically have to mention Cathy Henderson (the executive secretary) who served as my sounding board on so many occasions and often offered suggestions of her own.

To those others who doubted my ability to produce this book and said so, you challenged me and I responded to the challenge. Your words motivated me to prove my abilities. I hope that this book will motivate you also to remove the doubts that you possess about your own abilities. I hope that my accomplishments will show you that you too have the same power within you to achieve dreams beyond your imagination. Dream large and aim high and never doubt your abilities.

I specifically wish to acknowledge my sister Valerie who has always been a source of inspiration for me and constantly E-mails me with words of inspiration. The other members of my family have always provided me with support when I needed it and I thank them just as sincerely.

Finally, to all of my teachers, both living and dead, who contributed to the knowledge and wisdom that I have accumulated over the years, I hope that this book will serve as justification for your own efforts throughout the years to help someone else make a meaningful difference.

Teachers historically have never been adequately appreciated or rewarded for their efforts. Without the many teachers who have imparted their knowledge to me, I could not have produced the work that is in this book. If this book succeeds, I owe it all to my teachers. If it fails, the fault is entirely mine for not paying more attention to my teachers. By writing this book, this is my opportunity to repay a debt of gratitude to all my teachers, by sharing my own knowledge with others in the same way they did for me.

Time and space will not permit me to list the names of all those who imparted their knowledge to me. Therefore to everyone who had even the slightest contribution to my education, in whatever shape or form, thank you each and every one. Pay it forward.

Last but not least, I would like to thank Beverly Thompson who introduced me to her husband Pat Thompson and Carol Wajer of Diamond Computer Systems. Pat was responsible for doing an excellent job on the front cover of the book and the illustrations inside the book as well as helping me to prepare the manuscript for printing. To everyone I offer my sincere thanks.

The author welcomes your input at:
e-mail - **searsdoc@hotmail.com**

Dedications

This book is dedicated to my patients, for whom the book primarily was written and who have been my greatest sources of inspiration. I hope that the book will provide you all with hope for the future.

I also dedicate the book to the victims and families of the September 11th tragedy. I hope that this book will comfort you with the knowledge that change is the secret of life. Know that your sacrifice and that of your relatives was meant for us the survivors to take the opportunity to reform the world through seeking meaningful change. We can all use the lessons learnt from September 11th to make our world a better place.

In Memoriam

To my mother, Druscilla Martha Sita and to my late brother Walter, who sought and in the end found meaningful change and in the process showed me what true courage is and proved conclusively to me that it really is never too late to change.

Contents

Comments on the book

If your life, your relationship, your career or your business isn't going the way you want it, you need to read this book. If you want to take your business or organization to a higher level, read this book. If you are just looking for meaning to life, read this book.

This is a book about the meaning and the secret of life, your life and the life of every one else around you and in our world. It is a book about the life of your relationships, your business, your career, your institution, your organization and the society you live in. If you understand the principles in this book it will allow you to live the rest of your life to the maximum. You will learn that you too can accomplish all your dreams. It will restore power and control to you.

This book is intended to provide you with hope for the future. It is intended to restore hope to those who may have lost hope. The book is written in a manner so that you can read it in any order you wish, and yet be able to make sense of what you have read. You may start in the middle, at the end or in the beginning or you may simply look at the diagrams, which in themselves tell a whole story.

The principles in this book can help revive failing relationships or teach you how to start a lasting relationship. It can help you to revive a failing business or learn what it takes to succeed in business. It can teach you how to get your organization to grow. It will teach you how to get the maximum out of your employees and how to give the maximum of yourself. It will teach you how to deal with career burnout. It will also teach employees how to empower themselves so that they can find more job satisfaction.

It will help you learn how to cope with depression, anxiety, stress, rage, sexual dysfunction, obesity, smoking cessation and other medical conditions and help you to better manage your own health and the health of others.

I am confident that the content and style of this book are different from any other book on the market that has been written on the subject of change. Read this book and try to understand it and I assure you that it will make a huge difference in your life and help you to accomplish things that you never dreamed possible. Above all, it will help you achieve inner peace for yourself, as it has done for me.

This book will also bring peace to troubled lives. It will also allow us to understand the tragedy of Sept 11th 2001. Hopefully it will also allow us to prevent another September 11th, at least in our lifetime and our children's lifetime.

The author

<u>Disclaimer</u>

Throughout the book, where necessary, fictitious names have been used, to protect the privacy of individuals who may perceive a resemblance between certain situations and them. In those instances, the names are entirely fictional. They bear no resemblance to anyone living or dead and any resemblance to anyone living or dead is purely co-incidental.

CHAPTER 1

Introduction

Why **do** we change? Why **must** we change? Why do we **need to** or even **want to** change? The simple answer is, **'Because change is the essence of life!' Without meaningful change, growth ceases.**

To be more precise, the secret of life itself lies in change. Figure 1 clearly illustrates in graphic form that for any organism or organization or relationship that wants to grow or develop, change must occur. Without change, growth ceases and when this happens, decline and death of the organism or organization follows.

On closer scrutiny, we can see that this fact is true in **every** aspect of our lives and in our world whether that is as individuals, in our personal relationships, in our businesses and organizations or in our society. But **for growth and development to occur, change needs to be <u>meaningful</u>.**

Many individuals and organizations have acquired success because they learned to make meaningful change **instinctively**. Others must be **shown why** they need to and **how** to effect meaningful change. Failure to understand the **principles and process** of change is usually what causes many of these organizations and individuals to go into a state of decline and ultimately they fail.

When individuals, businesses and organizations that have previously been successful fail, it is usually as a result of the inability to <u>comprehend</u> the philosophy, principles and process of change and are unable to effect meaningful change.

Quality Farm and Fleet, one of the largest farm store retailers in the USA, after one of their most successful years suddenly announced the closure of all of its 153 stores nationwide. Just one year previously, Quality Farm and Fleet was the nation's largest farm store retailer. The steep slope of the downhill curve in Figure 1 could be used to illustrate the rapidity of the decline of this company. Clearly the decision to close had to have been unanticipated, since just one year previously, the Chief Operating Officer (COO) had predicted that, "in five years the company would be 600 stores and $2 billion in sales". The demise of this company was both sudden and extreme.

From understanding the philosophy of change and the principles behind the ability to effect meaningful change, it is clear that this company did not anticipate the need for, did not understand why they needed to or did not know how to effect meaningful change, which is absolutely essential for continued growth.

Unfortunately my book wasn't published soon enough to save this company but I am presumptuous enough to state that had my book been published earlier or had the directors understood the philosophy of change, it is quite possible that the company directors might have been able to see the need for meaningful change earlier on and could have taken appropriate steps to save this company.

Of equal interest is the fact that another company, Tractor Supply along with some others, has announced that it will purchase and reopen approximately 85 Quality Farm and Supply stores **but in their own format**.

This company clearly recognizes the need for change. It would be interesting to see if the new company is able to differentiate between meaningful changes and change per se. Only time will tell and we will know this if we follow the fortunes of the new company.

Why are people generally resistant to change? This can either be the result of **failure to recognize any benefits** to change or alternatively fear of the possibility of **loss**. **Change is not without risk**.

Others may **wish to change** and **recognize the need to change** but **lack of a clear vision** of the future prevents them from being able to make meaningful change. Others still may be able to see benefits to change, but are unable to **formulate a plan** or to be **able to implement their plan even when they do have one**. This book seeks to address all of these issues and is intended to offer **easy** solutions for dealing with the problems.

Change is a process and I have broken down the process into six easy and simple steps so that <u>anyone</u>, even those with an IQ of just greater than 50 can understand and follow the steps. And I do not intend to demean anyone; because I have taught this process to children as young as eight years old with full comprehension on their part and I am confident that the process can be taught to even younger kids.

I have discovered that the process of being able to effect meaningful change is so simple and the benefits are so great that I am flabbergasted that so many people are simply so unwilling to embrace change.

There are three possibilities to change. The first is change that results in decline or decay of the organism or organization. This is **negative** change. This type of change will result simply from being complacent or from neglect. Just the mere act of doing nothing will result in decay and decline.

In life when meaningful change ceases, the end result will be decline, decay and death. Put another way, when we cease to make meaningful change in our lives, stagnation sets in and decline followed by death is the ultimate result, whether that death is physical or mental or spiritual.

There is **a second type of change** that is often overlooked by many when they consider change. This is **short-term change**. This type of change is fleeting and does not result in any long lasting transformation of the organism or organization. This is the type of change that usually results from force or as a consequence of crisis. This is to be contrasted with meaningful change.

The third type of change **(meaningful change)** is change that **results in growth and development, the type of change for which we should all aspire**. This type of change requires the right blend of certain essential ingredients; just like plants need nutrients for growth and babies need nurture for their development.

The intent of this book is to address all of these issues and show people why they need to and how to make the meaningful changes necessary that will result in them fulfilling their goals and objectives and allow them to function to their maximum ability and to be able to enjoy life with the vitality and zest that it was meant to be.

After the tragedy of September 11th, the airline industry in an attempt to convey the impression that there was improved security for passengers started confiscating **toothpicks, and nail-clippers** and even scanning passengers' **shoes**- sometimes twice!

Yet anyone could walk into any Starbuck's Café **beyond the security checkpoints and purchase iced cappuccino in glass bottles.** *Any potential terrorist could walk into one of these Starbuck's Café and in full view of national guardsmen and other security agents, purchase their potential weapons and be served with a smile by the individual behind the counter.*

But it was even more ludicrous when I boarded one of these flights, very soon after the tragedy of September 11th and was offered a Pepsi Cola in an **aluminum can**. As I scanned the plane for potential terrorists **(like everyone else at the time, I had developed the psychic ability to identify potential terrorists just by looking at people)**, I could not help but wonder, "What if there are hijackers on board this flight, are they right now thanking the stewardess for offering them their potential weapons?"

I pointed out this incongruity to a member of the security services and asked that he bring the matter up with the relevant authorities. When I asked him what was the response, I was told that the issue was just shrugged off. *Obviously the focus was more on plastic knives and toothpicks and nail-clippers as potential terrorist weapons rather than glass bottles or aluminum cans.*

I thought of the national guardsmen patrolling the airports and thought to myself, **"This is not meaningful change!** Nothing has changed to improve security." I was proved right when about two months later, a terrorist slipped through the security screen with plastic explosives in his shoe and tried to set his shoe on fire. **Fortunately this individual had an IQ of less than fifty** or the results could have been disastrous.

While I was a boy growing up, there were stores that advertised **going out of business sales everyday**. The signs outside the stores read 'Big Savings' or ' 50% discount on everything in the store' or, 'everything must go,' day after day after day. I remember consciously making the decision to avoid those stores because I knew instinctively that the quality of their merchandise was not even worthy of being sold at flea markets. **Even the fleas would not buy from them**. The quality of their service and merchandise was so poor that they needed gimmicks to attract customers.

Today there are similar stores with signs such as " No down payment. No finance charges. No payments for the next **TEN YEARS!**" in their store windows. *Beware of these stores! You are likely to lose the shirt off your back or end up with stuff that even "Sanford and Son" would refuse.*

What I did not realize as a youngster **but my mother did**, was that these stores, in order to make up for the poor quality merchandise or poor quality of their service, were making **window-dressing changes** trying to convince customers that they were getting good deals.

These stores rarely thrived and there was usually a rapid turnover in ownership. Or else they profited at the expense of the working poor who were exploited by their high interest rates. And very often the type of clientele they attracted were those that **needed ten years of freedom from making payments anyway**.

In business, in our organizations, in our personal lives, these **window-dressing type changes** are solely intended to create the impression to others and us that significant changes are occurring. **These changes serve no purpose other than to satisfy our ego that some type of improvement has occurred or is occurring.**

An example of this is when corporations publish slogans extolling the values of their organization in the form of mission statements but fail to reproduce it in the quality of the service to their clients. In popular parlance, this is referred to as **'talking the talk but failing to walk the walk'**.

It is usually not very long before it becomes patently obvious to all and sundry that these changes serve no useful purpose to anyone other than the individuals who concoct the slogans. **These changes arise out of selfish interests or misguided motives**.

My mother recognized the poor quality of merchandise and poor quality service in these stores and never frequented them. She also discouraged us from going to these stores and I could never figure out why, as poor as we were (**with ten children in our family**), she never sought to take advantage of the **"bargains"** that these stores offered.

My mother was a very wise woman but I did not realize just how wise she was, until I undertook to study the principles and process of change. I do confess that when I was a struggling medical resident that I did once frequent one of these stores to purchase some furniture, much against my better judgment and in opposition to my mother's wise teachings.

When my older son was going off to college and I offered some of this same furniture to him for his dorm room, he politely declined and advised me that he could find better furniture amongst what other students had thrown out in the street for the garbage collector. Humility teaches wisdom!

Meaningful change is more than window-dressing change. **Meaningful change results in growth. Meaningful change is enriching. For change to be meaningful, the beneficiary of the change must experience positive and satisfying results**. When we discover and understand how to effect meaningful change in us and in others, the feeling and the power generated is greater than any words can describe adequately.

In the town that I live, there is a pharmacy called Healthway Pharmacy that thrives by doing its own compounding of medicines. **This pharmacy incorporates medicines into lollipops** so that little kids and older folks, who have difficulty swallowing pills or who spit up their medicines, will willingly take their medicines in the form of a lollipop. They also manufacture a suppository called, **"the rectal rocket,"** for treating people with inflamed hemorrhoids and other painful rectal conditions. These are examples of what I refer to as meaningful change.

Healthway Pharmacy was started in a little town called St. Charles and has recently expanded by opening a new store. I predict that with their innovative approach, they will soon grow and expand to other locations.

Rite Aid and CVS in the meantime have been closing large numbers of stores across the country. These large pharmaceutical chain stores have had greater success in selling beer and beauty supplies than in selling pharmaceuticals. I would not be at all surprised to see Healthway Pharmacy expanding to other towns and even major cities.

In one section of this book, I use the analogy of Tiger Woods as an example of what meaningful change is all about. Golf is a wonderful game for demonstrating many of the principles outlined in this book. It is often said (by golfers) that the game of golf is a microcosm of life.

It is a pity that the game is limited to the privileged few. I am happy to see the game being made more accessible to the less privileged and less talented (**me for example**). Learning and understanding the game of golf (I think) was one of the meaningful changes that **I** made in my life (**I still shank the ball in the water and get poison ivy from looking for balls in the woods but it has brought me an understanding of life like no other sport does**).

The intent of this book is to teach the process of how to effect meaningful change **in a simple and uncomplicated manne**r, to allow each and everyone of you readers the opportunity to explore your own talents to the maximum, whether in your personal life or in your organization.

This book explains the philosophy of change and teaches the process and principle of change and how to effect meaningful change <u>in every aspect of our life</u>.

I am confident that this book is different in both the content and style from other books that deal with the subject of change. It was my intent to be different so that I could be consistent with the theme of the book, which is meaningful change, as the title of the book suggests.

On a daily basis we see relationships that are failing or have failed. We see individuals who have fallen by the wayside and are lost to society. We see businesses that have failed. We see individuals and relationships and companies that merely lead an existence but are not alive.

This book is intended to help all those individuals, relationships, businesses and organizations that are failing or need to grow beyond their present position. Everyone should be able to see the potential for and the ability to achieve renewed growth. **This book has practical applications for every one and there is no one to whom this book would not have relevance.**

When individuals fail or personal relationships or businesses or organizations fail, the common thread is usually the **lack of meaningful change** within these individuals, their personal relationships, their businesses or their organizations. My study of the process revealed that the **same principles operate in every aspect of our lives**. And the rules remain the same.

Coca-Cola tried to change its formula in 1985 when sales were slumping. They even tried and reverted to reintroducing the original coke bottles for a short period of time. Meaningful change? No way!

I did purchase one of the <u>'new original'</u> coke bottles, as a collector's item and I still have the unopened bottle. Do I hear offers from a buyer out there? And while we are in the process of selling sunshine in a bottle, would you also like to buy my

beachfront property in Arizona? You are sure to find a lot of sand on my property but please remember to bring your own water.

Volkswagen, on the other hand, reintroduced the popular, 'Beetle' of the 1970's flower-power popularity. But before they did so, they made some improvements and upgrades to the vehicle. Meaningful change? That's right! What Volkswagen did was to take a good concept and make it better. Chrysler did the same thing when it reintroduced its PT Cruiser and it turned out to be a huge success.

These two examples illustrate a very important concept regarding meaningful change, which is that meaningful change does not mean that we must completely abandon whatever has worked well in the past. *It is remarkable how many people fail to grasp this simple concept when change is discussed.*

The 'Beatles', in their popular hit song, 'Hey Jude' summarized this aspect of change with the following lyrics:

'Hey Jude, don't be afraid.
Take a sad song and make it better.
The minute you let him into your heart,
Then you can start,
To make love better.'

And so, in the midst of the doom and gloom, with so many companies and individuals failing, we are still able to see other individuals, relationships, businesses, organizations, and societies thriving and growing and flourishing.

The question then has to be **"How do some people succeed while others just continue to drag themselves along in the dust of their decrepitude?**

Look around at some of the organizations in society today to see those that have grown and are thriving and those that are failing or see minimal growth!

If we take as an example the traditional churches, we see a major decline in the membership of these institutions. The Catholic Church, which was once one of the greatest organizations in the world, has seen significant decline in its membership. It has failed to grow and attract many new members to the congregation and it is failing to attract new members to the clergy.

Is this mere coincidence or is it just a reflection of the times we live in? I think not! *Because if it is that people are moving away from religion, then how come the evangelical churches are catering to standing room only congregations, week in and week out.*

Without wishing to be critical of any particular institution or organization, I suggest that *lack of meaningful change lies at the root of these failing institutions.*

Many of the traditional churches insist that they will not compromise their traditional values. I do not for one moment suggest that these institutions should divert from their core values but if there continues be a decline in both membership of their congregation and decline in individuals entering the ministry, how are they going to achieve their fundamental purpose, which is to spread the teachings of Jesus Christ.

And to whom are they going to spread the gospel; to half-empty church pews? Talk about preaching to the choir!

And why are women still looked upon as second-class citizens in these institutions. Are our institutions that much more different in their attitude to women than the former Taliban government in Afghanistan. I suggest that the difference is only relative.

I have a female patient **from one of the traditional churches** in my practice and she has just completed studies in the ministry. Her studies required her to be separated from her husband for significant lengths of time **simply because the opportunity for her to pursue these studies in the state in which she lived was extremely limited.**

She has since graduated and is an ordained minister in her church. I was told by the patient that **membership in her church is growing by leaps and bounds.** I consider the opportunity for her to become an ordained minister as meaningful change **but one that should have been forthcoming for years.**

Why are the evangelical churches growing by leaps and bounds? The reason they continue to grow is because they are not afraid to take on the **challenge of change.** They visualize a changing world, see a need for change and plan for and implement change in their organization. **They have made meaningful change and that is why they have grown.**

Many of the traditional churches remain rooted in rules and rituals that are applicable to the Medieval Age, fail to anticipate the need for change well in advance, are unwilling to accommodate change in a timely manner and when they grudgingly do make changes, often do not make meaningful change.

It is not my intention to be critical of the values of the traditional churches because I respect these institutions and wish to see them succeed. But I suggest that we can preserve the core values of these organizations and others and yet make those meaningful changes that will allow our organizations, businesses and relationships to grow **without compromising any of those values.**

The introduction of guitar music and saxophones into the traditional churches will not by itself result in significant improvement in attendance at these churches. Meaningful change will only result from a change of the **mental model** within which these organizations operate. And that change has to be an ongoing process to accommodate for ongoing societal changes.

Is it at all conceivable that our organizations and institutions can benefit from greater diversity among their leadership and membership? **Is it possible that we will ever change our mental model to accommodate a black person of quality as President of the United States or a woman or a Native American?** Heaven forbid that we should even **think** of a woman, far less a black woman or a Native American or Hispanic woman as president.

In the United States we pride ourselves in being such a progressive country and yet a woman has not even come close to being president (unless we count Monica Lewinsky.) Yet so called lesser-developed countries such as India and Sri Lanka have had women leading the government for what seems like eons.

Is it possible that we are depriving our organizations and institutions of even greater growth because of many of the fixed assumptions that we currently hold? The economists among us wil ask, **"Are we achieving pareto optimum?"**

Is it possible that if we change our mental model that we will then be able to make meaningful change and **exceed our wildest dreams in terms of our growth?**

The world is changing daily and there is no way we can stop the process nor can we reverse the process. We have to anticipate change, we must plan for change and we must understand **how** to implement change; **meaningful change** that is.

This book seeks to empower everyone to understand the doctrine of change and to understand the process; so that they can lead more fulfilling experiences and can achieve **maximal and continual** growth for themselves, their businesses, organizations and communities.

But the greatest benefit of understanding the principles and process of change is the opportunity for everyone to achieve a better understanding of <u>their purpose in life</u>.

Step up to the merry-go-round of change! The price of admission is only a dime's worth of <u>willingness</u> to embrace change!

Figure1

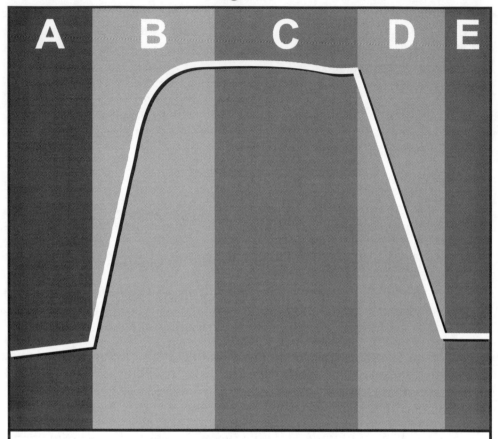

Diagram of the Product/Organism/Relationship/
Organization Life Cycle

A= Stage of Birth (origin).
B= Stage of Growth and Development.
C= Stage of Maturity (stagnation).
D= Stage of Decline and Decay.
E= Stage of Death (divorce, bankruptcy).

Upslope=Positive Growth
Downslope=Negative Growth
Flat=No Growth

CHAPTER 2

It's All About Meaningful Change

Writing this book has inspired me to thoughts and achievements that I never dreamed possible and I attribute it all to my study and understanding of the process of change.

Every single day that I have spent writing this book has inspired me to give more thought to the **"Process of Change"** and the result has been a spiritual awakening for me. It has opened my eyes to my inner soul, to my personal relationships, to my surroundings and to my world.

Preparing this book has also truly been a labor of love. It has given me great pleasure and great joy to prepare this book. It has been stimulating for me to devote hundreds of days of my free time and **every waking hour** to study and better understand the **meaning of meaningful change**.

The more I studied, learnt and applied the principle of change in my life and to the care of my patients, the more I became convinced of the need for another book such as this.

Whenever I mentioned to colleagues that I was writing a book on change, the most frequently asked question was, **"Do we really need another book like this?"**

The most appropriate response to this question is, **"Why don't you ask those patients who are experiencing the benefits of my teachings and who appreciate what a difference I have made in their lives, when everything else that they had tried previously had failed?"**

"Take a look at our society and the world we live in today and then tell me what limits we should set on books on change before people can learn and be taught how to eliminate negative and destructive behaviors from their lives!"

I am convinced that this book differs from every other book that has previously been written on the subject of change in both the content and style. That in itself is meaningful change; otherwise, I have wasted countless man-hours staying up late at night until the wee hours of the morning, wrestling with new ideas while writing this book and making change after change after change.

Thanks to the computer, I was able to revise this book over <u>sixty-five times</u> and

yet finish ahead of schedule. That is meaningful change. Without the computer I would probably still be on page five and I would have become so frustrated that I would probably have abandoned the project by now.

So many days, while driving along the highway or taking a casual walk somewhere, some exciting new thought or idea would pop into my head; or I would be walking along my hospital corridor and make an observation, which would inspire some profound thought and I would stop immediately and jot these thoughts down. If I did not, I found that it was very difficult to recall some inspiring ideas and observations.

With each success that I saw in my patients' responses to my teaching, I began to take a closer look at myself and **my** practice, my colleagues and **their** practices and I saw the crying need for meaningful change. I looked around at my surroundings, community and the organization for which I worked, and I saw this gaping void for meaningful change that cried out to be filled.

I became consumed with an almost obsessive desire to help others see the vision of hope and the benefits of change that I could see from my studies of the 'doctrine of change'; **this especially so since the United States and the world was just reeling from the catastrophe of September 11th.**

Because of the catastrophic events of September 11th, I could see that major changes would be **forced** upon our society but **I** had already learnt through my studies of the subject, to embrace change **willingly** and I understood that **change that is forced upon others is not meaningful change.**

Meaningful change only results when others can be shown why change is beneficial and teaching them how to effect meaningful change.

Every day, adversity and crises present us with the opportunity to extract lessons that could be used to learn how to effect meaningful change.

I could actually see many positives coming out of the horror of September 11th and I wanted to shout to Osama Bin Laden, **"Osama you miserable and pathetic fool, can't you see that you have failed? You sought to destroy us but you have only succeeded in making this country stronger than it has ever been and we will become the greatest country in the history of civilization!"**

I saw the **potential** for growth of our country and our world **to a level that we had never previously imagined** and I wanted to reassure everyone around me, **"Don't worry, we are going to be better than before, because we needed change and for growth to occur, change is necessary."**

Crisis results in connectedness as can be seen from the outpouring of support for the people of New York and the USA from within our own country and from

around the world.

Crisis can also result in chaos. But chaos itself results in creativity as I will demonstrate subsequently.

There are many lessons to be learnt from the events of September 11th. We as a nation and as a world felt a degree of connectedness as we had never seen before.

I wanted to reach out and hug every victim and every victim's family and reassure them **that their relatives did not die in vain and that out of the rubble of Ground Zero would arise a spirit of change that would make our world far greater and more humane than it ever was before.**

I wanted to reassure them that the events of September 11th would lead to a better world, one that **could** be so wonderful and great that we could never have imagined it in our wildest dreams and **that was the sacrifice of their relatives and friends.**

And in the aftermath of September 11th , I was reminded of another period when the world faced another crisis that occurred when the world was crying out for change. That was when God allowed the crucifixion of Jesus Christ so that our world could become a better place. **And so in the same manner, I do not believe that the victims of September 11th died in vain.**

But we all need to learn how to take the lessons from that disaster and apply them to effect meaningful change so that we as individuals and our entire society as a whole, can grow to levels previously undreamed of.

As for the chaos that follows any crisis, I am reminded of the following anecdote:

'There was once a little boy who was extremely well loved by his parents and other family members. There was nothing that he wanted that his family would not give him, as long as they could afford to do so.

One day, his parents bought him a hundred building blocks, which he used to build a beautiful house. He then asked them for and received another hundred blocks that he used to build another beautiful house. He repeated the request and was given another one hundred blocks and he repeated the process of building beautiful houses.

Eventually however, after his parents had bought his fourth one hundred blocks, they realized that they just could not afford to continue providing him with his requests for additional blocks and so when he put in his next request for an additional one hundred blocks, his parents refused.

This made the little boy so mad that he threw a tantrum and he proceeded to kick down every beautiful house that he had built. He sat around fuming for days.

19

After a while, he cooled off enough and looked around him and saw that he had four hundred blocks. He used those four hundred blocks to build the most beautiful castle, one that was more beautiful than any house that he had ever built. Out of the chaos, this little boy had developed a degree of creativity that he never knew lay within him.'

Similarly I firmly believe that out of the chaos of September 11th, such a degree of creativity <u>could</u> emerge that the USA and the other nations of the world together could build a world that we never would have imagined in a million years.

The more I studied and applied the principles of change as I had conceived and developed them, the greater skilled I became in developing a mastery for the subject and for the application of the process and with each success that followed, a blazing fire was fueled within me that convinced me that I was on a mission and I was determined to fulfill that mission.

Teaching others how to effect meaningful change has become my mission in life.

I observed my colleagues and the people that I dealt with on a daily basis and I saw the need to help others see why change is essential. With my study and increasing knowledge of the process of meaningful change, I realized that **we all have the capacity to make meaningful change in us and in others and we have the capacity to teach others how to learn the process. But more than that, we have a moral obligation** to help others learn the process.

The more I refined the process of teaching others how to effect meaningful change, the greater success I achieved and I was more and more determined to fill that gaping void that needed to be filled in my patients' lives, in my institution and in our society. Absolutely nothing was going to prevent me from fulfilling my newfound mission.

The tools for teaching others the process of change were first acquired through participation in a Physician Leadership program sponsored by the American College of Physician Executives. I took those tools, honed them and refined them for my own purposes.

But the <u>inspiration</u> to write the book came from the hundreds of patients that I was treating week in and week out with essentially the same problem, i.e. their inability to effect meaningful change in their lives. My patients encouraged and drove me to continue writing this book through their urgency to see the finished work.

Through introspection, I recognized that the first thing that I needed to do was to change me, my practice habits and my perception of life and the first change I made was a conscious decision to **get rid of all of the fixed assumptions** that I previously held about every thing that I had previously been made to believe was true.

Learning to abandon my fixed assumptions was a dramatic point in my life and

the pivotal point in my own change.

The Physician Leadership program stimulated me to start thinking in abstract and philosophical terms and to move away from the concrete thinking to which I had previously been accustomed. The result of my participation in that program was what is referred to as a paradigmatic shift.

I abandoned all my previously held assumptions about everything that I had learnt in medical school and opened my mind to a clean slate of thoughts. The effect on me was dramatic.

I instantly recognized that the limitations that I had placed on myself in terms of my mental growth were as a result of many of the fixed assumptions that I previously held.

Suddenly I began questioning everything about the practice of medicine and about my perception of my own abilities. I became able to visualize potential achievements as I had never done before.

I recognized that it was the <u>fixed assumptions</u> that most people held that limited their ability to visualize change or to implement change.

This lack of understanding of how to effect meaningful change was pervasive in many professionals including physicians as well as patients. It was simply amazing how many **negative assumptions** are held by so many and how many people resign themselves to accept that particular situations in their lives and the lives of others and in their surroundings just cannot be changed except through the intervention of outside forces, if at all. *I recognized that meaningful change comes from within us.*

Consequently these individuals accept grudgingly, whatever limitations fate and their **own** fixed assumptions impose upon them and they then complain bitterly about their sad misfortune. They develop what I refer to as the **'Oh woe is me attitude.'**

I remember only too well, a comment made by one of my colleagues, a neurologist, in my hospital, over lunch, regarding some very basic projects that I was proposing for improvements in the hospital.

In studying the process of change, I recognized that through some very basic changes in our operations we could make significant improvements in the quality of care in our institution.

Not only would the quality of care improve but also the resultant **savings** and potential for **increased revenue** could be enormous, possibly in the millions of dollars.

My proposals were in no way earth-shattering, involved minimal risk and would be very simple to implement. The results of implementing these simple proposals would likely be **huge cost savings** in some areas, **improved quality of care** in every area and

marked improvement in revenue in terms of millions of dollars to the hospital.

But because he himself could not visualize the end results of the proposed changes, his comment was that we needed to be careful about having unrealistic dreams. I had to inform him that **our achievements in life were only limited by how great our dreams were.**

After all, as I reminded him, it was not too long ago that the prevailing belief was that man could never walk on the moon. **In fact, there are still some who believe that the moon is made of blue cheese! I didn't dare ask him for his opinion on the make up of the moon's surface.**

But as I also informed him, we just might soon be sending people to live on Mars **(as soon as we have destroyed Mother Earth through our negative and destructive behaviors)!**

In the medical field it is equally astonishing how many of our patients simply assume that there are no alternatives and are willing to take the many noxious drugs that are being foisted upon them by physicians and 'health food charlatans' simply because so many physicians and patients fail to understand the concept of meaningful change.

The patients who really are seeking change are themselves unable to see how they can implement the meaningful changes that would allow them to enjoy a better quality of life They seek guidance from their physicians. **Instead of pointing them to an oasis in the desert, we as physicians offer them sips of water from a cactus (in the form of pills) and then allow them to continue to wander in the desert.**

I will address the devastating economic implications of this type of behavior in a later section of the book.

When I looked around me at my community and my institution and our organizations, it was glaringly apparent that the same problems and attitudes and behaviors permeated our entire society!

In spite of the numerous self-help books out there, it was astounding how deficient was our understanding of the principle and process of change. The simple fact is that many of the existing books on change are so complex that the man in the street has great difficulty grasping the concept.

When I examined some of the books that dealt with the subject of change, one glaring fact that struck me was that **I could not recall a single book addressing the subject of 'meaningful change versus change per se'. It struck me like a bolt of lightning that if people could not differentiate between meaningful change versus any old type of change, that it should come as no surprise where our problems lay.**

The motivation for writing this book also arose from the fact that day in and day out I found myself treating patients for the same type of problems and realizing that these people had not been helped by existing books on the subject.

I realized that my colleagues faced similar frustrating problems as I did. By extrapolation if we look at the worldwide community, it horrifies me to think that there are millions of individuals, personal relationships, businesses and possibly thousands of organizations that are crying out for simple solutions as to how to effect meaningful change and are unable to find simple answers.

Would the multitude of problems that exist in the world today be present if this were not so?

In dealing with the numerous patients in my practice it was glaringly apparent that their biggest problems were the fixed assumptions that many of them held, from the ideas that they could not lose weight without a pill, to the idea that a pill would cure their depression or make them quit smoking, improve their sex life, treat their phobias and resurrect their failing relationships.

Assumptions by themselves are self-limiting and inhibit your potential to be innovative. Fixed assumptions on the other hand are not only self-limiting but also inhibiting and regressive.

I instantly realized that if people were going to be helped, the first priority would be to help them **get rid of some of their most fundamental assumptions** regarding their inability to effect change.

With each couple and individual that I helped solve their problems, the more glaringly apparent it became, of the need for this type of book. Although I was helping patients individually and helping couples with their relationships, I found it extremely time-consuming and an **inefficient use of my time**.

I realized that if I was going to get my message of how to effect meaningful change to as many people as possible in the most efficient, time saving manner, it would be necessary to put my thoughts in writing.

Moreover, **a book can always be used for reference and reinforcement** of the principles that I was employing and I realized that in spite of the positive effects that I was achieving with these patients, they **would** need constant reinforcement.

When my patients realized that I intended to write a book, they not only encouraged me to do so, **they positively insisted that I get it out as soon as possible. And I felt I had an obligation to them to do so having introduced them to the concept of change.**

The more I promoted my philosophy to colleagues and friends and anyone who cared to listen; the enthusiasm with which they embraced my ideas convinced me that I had something worthwhile to contribute.

The enthusiasm with which they embraced my philosophy and the urgency with which they anticipated my book drove me to go home at night, even when I was dog-tired, to desperately seek to get this book out for them as soon as possible.

Having studied, learnt and understood the concept of change and why change was necessary and how to implement meaningful change, I became determined every day to pursue and to apply the principles into my medical practice and to seek mastery of the skills. The transformation on my life and to my practice was both immediate and dramatic.

I could not believe the amazing transformation on both my patients and me. I was suddenly able to convince my patients; **even the most "noncompliant"** ones to make drastic lifestyle changes. The changes were equally applicable in helping them deal with **depression and anxiety** as it was in assisting them with **weight loss, smoking cessation, diabetic management, hypertension, sexual dysfunction, phobias, managing their heart disease and virtually every aspect of their medical care.**

What also became apparent, was the realization that as my patients benefited from their newfound attitude towards their health, I too was gaining both directly and indirectly from dealing with a **healthier** group of patients. In a managed care setting, this is a win-win situation for all concerned, including the managed care organizations.

With meaningful change, everyone is a winner. There are no losers when meaningful change occurs.

My own sense of self-fulfillment also improved. The effect on me was even more dramatic than the effect on my patients. Suddenly, my attitude to medical practice was buoyant and upbeat. I recovered my "joie de vivre". I had myself changed and I was making meaningful change in my patients' lives.

Suddenly I had recovered the autonomy and power that I had previously been resigned to turn over to the HMO's and Government regulators and other third party payers.

Words cannot explain the excitement that I felt and the power that surged through me when I regained the autonomy that I wanted in my life and which I had long ago discarded as fantasy. I had regained control of my personal life and my practice and words cannot express the excitement and the power that I felt in being in control of my own destiny.

As I will explain in a later section of this book, *it is that lack of control or the feeling of not being totally in control or relegating control to someone else, plus the perception of being unable to effect meaningful change in specific situations, that is the underlying basis of anger, phobias, anxiety, frustration and depression.*

What a difference in our world it would make if we could help people who suffer chronically from these problems, if we could teach them how to channel their energies into learning how to effect meaningful change.

We could prevent future school shootings such as happened at Columbine High School. We could prevent so many suicides among our youth and elderly. We could reduce the use of costly and harmful drugs, both prescription and non-prescription, that is so prevalent in our society.

I know what the drug dealers and pharmaceutical companies are saying at this point. "We are going to be put out of business". Not so I say! In another section of the book, I will show the tremendous economic benefits to meaningful change, for all of us. Instead of fighting for crumbs at the table as so many pharmaceutical companies are doing, they could each be looking to see where they could get a bigger share of another pie. The opportunities are there. They just have to demonstrate the willingness to embrace change.

We could save billions of dollars in healthcare costs, money that could be channeled into providing medical coverage for the **millions in our own country and billions in the world, who are without adequate medical coverage**. We could have a better society because of fewer broken homes.

We could even avoid the frustration of watching our favorite football or basketball or hockey teams, losing week in and week out.

But most of all, we could avoid other September 11ths if we could teach the Osama Bin Ladens of this world why it is necessary and how to go about effecting **meaningful change** without indulging in the destructive fanaticism that fuels their cause.

Maybe there is hope after all that Israel and Palestine can co-exist in peace and harmony. **If it would make a difference, I will send a free copy of this book to the Prime Minister of Israel and the leader of the Palestine Liberation Army, if they will promise to read the book! Otherwise they will have to purchase it just like everyone else.**

When I realized that not only could **I** change myself but I also had the knowledge to share my newfound power with others, it struck me immediately that I had more than the opportunity to help others effect meaningful change in their lives.

I recognized that I had a moral obligation to help others understand the process. This further stimulated and stoked my interest and desire to continue with this book.

But I also recognized that change does not come easily and meaningful change is not a one time effort but an ongoing effort and it requires a lot of dedication on the part of the individual who is teaching change, as well as the subjects of change.

The additional incentive for me to continue writing this book, was when I realized that **I, not unlike so many of my colleagues, had been very deficient in my techniques in treating patients and it hurt me to the point of tears when I recognized that we as clinicians had been practicing, literally, poor quality medicine for many years.**

We were practicing nineteenth century medicine in a twenty-first-century setting. This in spite of the fact of all the newer technology and newer medicines!

It brought tears to my eyes one day, when I realized how much hurt I, not unlike so many of my colleagues, had brought to our patients. Of course we had not done this consciously or deliberately. As clinicians we all are well intentioned but the truth was that we didn't have a clue how to effect meaningful change in our lives, far less in our patients' lives.

If we have not learnt how to effect meaningful changes in our own practices, how can we expect to help our patients effect meaningful change in their lives? **Can the blind lead the blind? Rather I should ask, "Can the dead lead the blind?"**

Humpty Dumpty

'All the king's horses and all the king's men, couldn't put Humpty together again.'

During the course of examining one of my patients, a young housewife and mother and a wonderful person, I realized that this poor soul had been allowed to suffer for eight horrible years (for her). And within half an hour, using my newly learnt technique, I was able to address her real needs through my understanding of the doctrine of the need for meaningful change.

It was embarrassing to me that I could not control the tears that came to my eyes, right there in front of that patient, when I recognized how terribly inefficiently that person had been treated and allowed to suffer by both her physicians and the professional counselors she had seen over an eight-year period. I fought hard to withhold the tears but simply couldn't.

The only solution this beautiful and trusting person could get to help her with her problems was a prescription for pills; either I felt, because no one recognized the need for changes in her life, or alternatively they did not care, which I know was far from the truth.

I knew that she had seen some of the finest physicians in our community. **These were physicians who cared!** Yet this poor patient had been allowed to suffer for eight years with the trash-basket diagnoses of anxiety and depression and the way we have become ingrained to treat these conditions!

So where was the problem that would allow this to happen to our patients day in and day out?

The harsh realization dawned on me, that all the physicians and counselors she had seen over the course of eight years, plus her primary care physicians (as well as the patient herself), really did not understand the philosophy of change and **how to help others effect meaningful change**.

If they did, then why was I needing to devote so much of my time to addressing problems that the psychologists and psychiatrists should have been dealing with.

I thought of the millions of other patients that we had failed because of our failure to understand a simple concept of how to effect meaningful change and to effectively help those people to understand that concept. Such a simple concept can have such a huge effect in making major differences in people's lives.

I thought of my own brother who had died of alcoholism, **because I, my family, his friends, his physicians and the psychologists and psychiatrists who treated him did not understand the principles of how to effect meaningful change in others. Oh how I wish that I knew then what I know now!**

I thought of the millions of broken families that we as physicians had an opportunity to help and those who we had failed miserably. I thought of the millions of drug addicts and alcoholics that we could have helped but didn't. I thought of the millions of patients that we label day after day as non-compliant and refuse to treat, all because of our own failure to effectively project a simple concept to our patients.

I felt anger, frustration and shame at my past deficiencies and that of my colleagues and the tears came rolling from my eyes right in front of the patient. When I felt the needless hurt these patients had undergone, I just could not control the tears.

I apologized to the patient for what appeared to be a moment of weakness. But I became more resolved there and then that I was going to share my ideas with as many others as possible.

I had changed but more importantly, I understood what it took to help others effect meaningful change. I resolved there and then that I was going to commit myself to helping as many others as possible to see the need for change and to help them learn how to effect meaningful change.

That particular patient was so grateful that she hugged me and thanked me when she left the office and I knew right away that I had made a meaningful change in that person's life.

My only regret was that it had taken her so many years to finally come up with a solution to her problems. Since then I have treated so many others who have spent so many needless years of suffering all because we as physicians never fully understood the process of change.

I applied the same principles of change with other patients. Suddenly, my patients were leaving my office and hugging me and expressing their gratitude. In one day, five patients spontaneously hugged me and thanked me for the help I had given them to help effect meaningful changes in their lives.

I could not remember being hugged for many years by a patient even when I had successfully operated and cured them or a loved one of cancer. (I was a surgeon before I **changed** and became a Family Physician).

Looking Into The future From 1998

Changes in warfare became apparent during Operations Just Cause and Desert Storm, and the Army began changing in order to take advantage of the international change, the bow wave of technology that marked the onset of the Information Age, and the military reductions that were imposed to accommodate a lesser threat. indeed, during the years after the Cold War and into the new century, the Army has been focused on change

-change in the way we do business, change in the way we change.

General William W. Hartzog
"American Military Heritage

As seen in the above quotation from a brilliantly written book on American military history by General William Hartzog, even the military recognized the need for meaningful change. How else could we have managed to suffer so few casualties in the wars against Iraq and in Afghanistan?

Nausea? What Nausea

I remember the change in attitude of one of my patients with an infectious disease, from one of suicidal thoughts towards herself and homicidal feelings towards her former partner (from whom she had contracted the disease), to one where she was so charged up with her newfound power that she was going right out to treat herself at Red Lobster. This patient whom I shall call Violet had come to my office **wanting medicine for her nausea and poor appetite**. She had been diagnosed with an infectious disease and was referred back to me by the specialist to whom I had originally referred her because the doctor recognized that she was depressed.

In spite of the fact that she was being treated with some of the newest and most expensive medications and had an excellent prognosis, she was extremely frustrated and angry with her former husband.

She related to me how her memory was being affected and how on one occasion in the recent past she had found herself about one hundred and fifty miles away from her intended destination heading towards the Mackinac Bridge in Michigan, when her intended destination was only ten minutes away from where she started.

She was scared that something was seriously wrong with her and wondered whether the medicines that she was taking were causing her to have side effects or whether the disease was responsible for her symptoms. My first inclination was to think that maybe some of her medicines were indeed causing her problems and offered a pill to counter her nausea.

But after further questioning I observed the anger and hostility that was emerging towards her former husband. At one point she angrily retorted, *"Doctor Sears, you don't know how angry I am at that man! I feel like I could kill him for what he has done to me! Do you know that one day at the gas station, I threw gasoline on him and the only thing left for me to do was to light the match? I wanted to kill him and kill myself for him destroying my life! Only the good Lord prevented me from doing it because he knows I would never do such a thing! I wasn't brought up that way!"*

I was shocked and aghast! Here was this formerly benign, pleasant, soft-spoken, charming patient, expressing such violent feelings towards her ex-husband. A light bulb went on in my head instantly. I recognized what the problem was immediately.

It was instantly apparent to me that all of this patient's symptoms were related to the bitterness and anger and frustration that was boiling up inside of her like the Mount Pele volcano ready to erupt violently. **It was interesting to compare her with an erupting volcano because the nausea that was causing her stomach to churn was so very similar to the violent upheavals in the belly of a volcano.**

After soothing her feelings towards her husband, I reassured her that her disease was well controlled and that her prognosis was excellent. I then suggested to her that **she was living in the past** and she was allowing the past and the anger that she felt towards her husband, to eat away at her insides.

In keeping with my philosophy of teaching meaningful change, I then suggested to her that I could help her deal with her problems in a more meaningful manner and walked her through the six steps in the process of change (**which are outlined in subsequent sections of this book**). It was as if a light bulb had exploded inside her head. She leaned forwards towards me, eyes wide and shining and exclaimed, "Doctor Sears, **you** know **what**? You know what? You are so right! **You are so very right!** All along I was letting that man destroy my life! I am going to show him that he cannot destroy my life! I am going to take charge of my own life from now on. Thank you doctor! Thank you so very much!"

Violet gave me the nicest hug I had ever had and seeing her newfound vibrancy, I encouraged her to go out and do something nice for herself. I encouraged her to go out and treat herself. Her response was, **"That's right! I am** going to treat myself **very nicely** right now!"

When I asked her how she was going to treat herself, Violet responded, **"I am going to Red Lobster of course!" Remember that this was a lady who had come in to me for medications for nausea!** As she was leaving, I reminded her that I was going to write a prescription for her nausea. Her response was, "Nausea? What nausea? You just showed me that there is nothing wrong with me. I don't need any medicines. **I just can't wait to taste those delicious crab legs!"**

You cannot imagine the satisfaction that a physician gets when patients feel satisfied with their care and show their gratification. The hugs that I received that day and subsequently, were more than expressions of gratitude. Those hugs are recognition and my reward for a job well done.

When I see the hurt and pain in the patients faces as I enter the examination rooms and during the interview I become more and more resolved to implement the techniques that I have learnt and to help as many others as possible to learn how to apply the same techniques in their lives.

And when I see the hope in their eyes when they leave my office, the transformation is absolutely fantastic and complete and I am filled with joy myself. I no longer leave my office mentally fatigued at the end of the day. I feel more energetic and mentally recharged. **I am physically fatigued because I am working harder but I am actually enjoying myself in medical practice again.**

By writing this book, I recognized that it was possible to accomplish better results in a more efficient manner and to help a greater number of people at the same time. **As stated previously the written word serves the purpose of being available for reference purposes and also for reinforcement** of some of the techniques and principles that are outlined in this book.

Like my patients, I became filled with hope for the future!

Managed Care would never again be my Nemesis. I would never again feel threatened or be bothered by managed care. I determined that it would never again be a thorn in my side like it was with so many of my colleagues. **I could even see the need and the opportunity to make meaningful change in the managed care organizations themselves.**

Quite frankly, I now welcome managed care more enthusiastically into my practice. I instructed my staff and some of my colleagues that I was never ever again going to turn away anyone from my practice. **I was willing to accept anyone that everyone else had rejected from his/her practice.**

I was willing to accept the most **"non-compliant"** patients. If I truly believed in my philosophy, I should be able to take the very worst patients and help them to see the benefits of change and to help them to change and become the best patients. This in fact makes sound economic sense, especially in a managed care setting.

My patients have become winners and I became a winner. Still it bothers me tremendously when I realize that so many other patients are being deprived of best quality care and so many of my colleagues are disenchanted with their careers.

Virtually every physician I have spoken with in recent times is disenchanted with the profession. In fact as a member of the board of directors of the Michigan Academy of Family Practice, one of the first issues we were confronted with was the decline in interest in Family Practice.

But from my own observations, the problem went far beyond Family Practice and Primary Care. Across the board, it was apparent that there was an overall decline in interest in medical school applicants as a whole. Potential physicians were being encouraged to go into business. **Yet the business people were themselves complaining about how poorly they were doing.** After all, at the time of writing of this book, the United States was in a recession and may still be in a recession by the time I finish writing it.

At the time of writing of this book, many of the technology companies had already gone through their boom period and were now busted. Enron, one of the largest energy companies had gone bankrupt. Over seven hundred thousand people (in the USA alone) had lost their jobs within a very short period of time. By the time I am finished writing this book, the number is likely to exceed one million. So what hope could we offer the youth of today or the youth of tomorrow?

The answer surprisingly is simple and lies in the need for us to visualize change and how to effect meaningful change, the change that would allow our organizations and businesses and our world to enjoy renewed growth, to a level previously unseen! The philosophers call this **'inventing your future'**.

Through my understanding of the principles and process of change, I have developed nothing but a positive outlook for the future. I am able to look forward to the future because I can see a future that is full of promise and hope.

Despite all the doom and gloom that permeates our society, I have seen my own practice booming and my personal satisfaction increase tremendously! I became convinced that not only could I invent my own future; it was necessary and possible to teach others how to do the same. I foresaw a need and an opportunity to spread my message of change and I determined to do this by putting my thoughts in writing in the form of a book.

Through studying, learning and understanding the principles and process of

change, I took my techniques of enacting change to my hospital. Suddenly, I found that I was able to influence nurses and administrators.

I saw the capacity for making significant changes in my hospital. Suddenly I had power equal to that of the CEO of my institution to be able to effect meaningful change without anyone feeling threatened in their job, including the administrators. The fact is that every individual in any type of organization has equal power as any other to effect meaningful change. *This is what is meant by empowerment.*

We see so many mission statements of companies and organizations extolling the principle of empowerment. And yet, so often we hear individuals blaming the administration or others in authority for some failure in their institution with statements such as, *'the administration doesn't know what it is doing.'*

We willingly assign all responsibility for everything that happens to us, to those in authority, refusing to accept that we all have the power to influence change. We allow others to invent our future and then we complain when that future is not what we wanted. I will illustrate this point further in the section titled, 'The power to influence change.' *The ability to influence meaningful change is what empowers us and we can all have that power.*

When we understand fully the concept of how to effect meaningful change, we recognize that meaningful change can only lead to win-win situations. Every one wins with meaningful change. There are no losers. We do not require the permission of any other person to empower us to make meaningful change, unless we live under communist regimes.

I have become a futurist thanks to Leland Kaiser, one of the greatest philosophers I have ever encountered. I had already become a disciple of Lee Kaiser. Through Lee Kaiser, I learnt how to view the world without blinders on. I developed an **"open "mental model** for myself, as opposed to the **"closed" mental model** within which I had been operating previously. These terms will be explained in more detail in later sections of this **book.**

Through introspection I saw a mental model of myself that needed to be changed. **I looked at my relationships with my patients, my organization, my community, my country, my world and my personal relationships and understood why I needed to change, how to change, how to help others change and how change benefits all of us collectively.**

As a result, within a short time span I have achieved more with my patients than I had previously accomplished in 27 years of medical practice. I also found myself with the ability to make and influence meaningful change in my organization and my community. And through an understanding of the powerful effects of change, I found a new spirituality that brought new meaning to my life.

I listened to the Reverend Billy Graham during one of the memorial services after the World Trade Center bombing and he spoke of the need for a reaffirmation of our spirituality. I knew then, as I know now, that the only way we will accomplish this is through meaningful changes in our lives.

Every time we are faced with crisis, we are apt to ask why God would want us to endure such crises. The answer lies in the need for us to change but we never do so until crisis forces us to change.

But as I have stated before and as I will show in later sections of this book, **forcing others to change does not result in meaningful change. Force only results in short-term change. Meaningful change is long lasting and enduring**.

When I see the amount of despair among my patients, among my colleagues, in my institution and in society, I realize the need for a book to help give others hope for a brighter future.

And when I apply the principles of change in my own life, in my care for patients and in my organization, it is apparent that **I** have as much capability to make a huge difference. I also have the need to, the opportunity and the capacity to share my knowledge with everyone else. **Together we can make a huge difference**.

As the title of the chapter states, 'It's all about change', i.e. changing ourselves, our approach to personal relationships, our attitude to our careers, our relationships with our organizations and our communities and more than anything else, **our relationship with our spiritual self.**

By making a conscious effort to "change", I realized that I had the ability to make a major difference in every aspect of my life. **But more than my own self-interests**, I see the opportunity to help **others** effect meaningful change in their lives, their relationships, their organizations and in their communities and society.

The ability to effect meaningful change leads to reduced stress and anxiety and frustration through greater control of one's circumstances and environment.

Everyone can be and needs to be taught how to effect meaningful change so that they can feel a greater sense of being in control in their lives. When we achieve these objectives, we will have a more productive society. We will also reduce the anger and frustration, anxiety and depression and feeling of hopelessness that exist in our society today.

By teaching people how to effect meaningful change in their lives, we are empowering them to take control of their lives. When these individuals have greater control, they are apt to accept more responsibility for themselves and their creativity comes to the forefront. **This way, the whole society benefits.**

We each and every one of us have the capacity to change and to help others change. We **must** change for growth to take place in us as individuals, in our organizations and in our society. **We must also change for spiritual growth to occur**.

The ability to change our selves and help others to implement change results in tremendous power that extends far beyond our imagination. That power puts us in control of our lives. **We are no longer at the mercy of others. We have the capacity to invent our own future and not let others invent a future that we might not care for**. This is a feeling that words cannot describe.

I have a newfound purpose in life. Life has become invigorating again. I now look for every opportunity where I could help to make meaningful change. I have planned to continually invent my own future and I wish to help others to do the same.

I am determined and resolved to share my knowledge with as many people as possible and I recognize that the best way for me to accomplish this is by putting my thoughts in writing.

I realize that the more people I succeed in helping to understand the concept of "change" and its implications, the better positioned would be our society and our world. This way, we can all be winners.

I also understand that one of the main reasons people resist change has to do with the fact that there is an element of risk in change. People are generally afraid of any risk involved in a change of the status quo. But without risk there is little chance of reward.

In this book, I use philosophical terms such as **"mental model"**, **"inventing one's future" "open systems"** and **"closed systems"** and other such terms. These terms are explained by definitions and by using examples to illustrate the meaning of the terms. I also use psychological terms and principles for illustrating how to influence change. I also utilize economic and marketing terms and principles to illustrate how to implement change.

But I will attempt to simplify these terms and use diagrams so that <u>anyone</u> reading this book will understand and be able to apply the principles described within.

When I decided to participate in a physician leadership program, it was as a result of an instinctive desire to implement change in my own life. I was seeking change in my own life without fully being aware at the time of why I needed to change. I simply knew that I wanted to do something different but I couldn't quite figure out why or how.

Before this, I had given up a successful career as a General Surgeon to become a Family Practice physician. It was not until I started to think in philosophical terms, that I understood **my** need to change and why **everyone else** needs to and can be taught how to effect meaningful change in his/her life and **why change has to be an ongoing process**.

It was not until after I learnt to think in abstract terms that I realized the profound effects that my understanding of the philosophy of change would have on not only **my** life but also the lives of everyone that I came in contact with.

I have become a disciple of change. I am a student of change. I am an agent of change. My wish is to recruit others to do the same. **We can all benefit from learning how to effect meaningful changes in our lives.**

The principles and concepts outlined in this book are equally applicable to individuals, to personal relationships, to organizations, to communities and to whole societies. I hope that all those who read this book will use the information to apply practically in all aspects of their lives.

I hope that this book will inspire others to change and to become students and agents of change. I believe that you will find an exciting world of opportunity out there.

If this book inspires just one person to make a change in her/his mental model, I will have succeeded because I know that one individual has the power to change many others and ultimately we can change the world.

> 'To change and to change for the better, are two completely different things.'
> **Old German Proverb**

CHAPTER 3

The Evolution of Change

Figure 1

Anyone who has studied marketing would recognize Figure 1 as representing the **Product Life Cycle**. I have shown this graph to many students of marketing and their immediate response is, "I know what that is!" When I ask them what it represents, their response is, "the product life cycle of course." Yet when I explain that this same diagram also represents the **Evolution of Change as it applies in every aspect of our lives, the comment elicits puzzled and quizzical looks from the vast majority.**

If ever anyone doubted that "Change is the essence of life", then Figure 1 should remove all doubts. If we examine the evolution of any **organism, individual, personal relationship, business, institution, organization, community, society, our world**, we will see that the path of development is identical to the graph in figure 1.

This graph, which in marketing represents the **'product life cycle'**, is actually the **'cycle of life changes'. Why is it that when I have shown this graph to students of marketing it is instantly recognized as the product life cycle but yet they fail to see that it represents anything else with any remote connection to other aspects of their lives? Maybe the answer lies in the fact that no one else has ever sought to explain the philosophy of change in a graphical form such as seen in Figure 1.**

As **individuals**, we are born and slowly go through infancy (A). We then go through the phase of rapid growth and development, (adolescence) and then growth reaches a peak throughout early adulthood (B). This is followed by the stage of maturity when growth slows and then ceases in middle and late adulthood (C). This is followed by the phase of decline in our older years (D) until finally we die (E)

When we examine **relationships**, it is clear that the evolution of a relationship is identical to the growth of individuals.

First there is the introduction of the two parties followed by a period of early courtship when the relationship slowly develops (A).

This is followed by the explosive growth of the relationship as the relationship blossoms (B) during which time marriage may follow. The relationship matures as children are produced and may follow the course in (C).

If things begin to sour, then the relationship may follow the path in (D), during which there is a decline in feelings towards each other. If this path is allowed to go unchecked, the ultimate outcome is (E), i.e., death of the relationship or divorce.

In **business**, marketing principles teach that this graph is referred to as the product cycle. When a new product is introduced to market, the life cycle of the product will follow the same course outlined in the graph.

When a new product is introduced to market, there is the initial phase of introducing the product to the market and getting the consumer familiarized with the product (A). Growth at this stage may be gradual as the consumers gradually become familiarized with the product.

If the product takes off in the public's imagination, the sales of the product follow (B). As the market becomes saturated with the product, the path of its sales follows (C). With flattening of sales and loss of the novelty of the product or the emergence of a competitor, sales follow a downward trend (D) and eventually, the product is off the shelves (E).

If we look at our **organizations**, our **institutions**, our **communities**, our **society**, the picture remains the same. Look at the Roman Empire and the Greek Civilization and you will see the same course as outlined in the graph in figure 1.

Look at the once mighty British Empire and see where Britain stands in relation to the rest of the world today. **Remember when 'Britannia ruled the waves'?** If we examine every one of these societies, the picture remains consistent. Isn't this what happened to the once mighty Russian Empire?

If this is the natural course of change, is it possible to avoid what appears to be a natural process of decline and decay and ultimately death. How can a country such as the United States avoid what appears to be the inevitable?

That is precisely the type of answer that this book seeks to provide. The short answer is that we need to learn how to effect meaningful change in our society on a continual basis so that we as a society can continue to grow.

Anyone who believes that they can continue to develop and grow without seeking to make meaningful change, whether that be in their relationships or their businesses or their organizations, is not only misguided but just plain **dumb**.

It doesn't matter whether you are Bill Gates, Ted Turner, Warren Buffet, Donald Trump, Bill Cosby, Oprah Winfrey, Jay Leno or the TV show, 'Who Wants To Marry The Bride From Hell'; if you do not understand the need for meaningful change, you are heading down the slippery slope of decline and decay.

Using the examples of Nintendo and Game Boy and Beanie Babies, **even little children can be made to understand these concepts.**

Physicians will also recognize that the graphic representation in Figure 1 represents the growth, development and decline of individuals, from birth to death, that is the human growth curve.

Businessmen will recognize that this represents the **product life cycle**. Politicians will recognize that this represents the course of development of their political parties.

World leaders will recognize that this graph represents the course of nations. Television producers recognize when they need to develop new programs for TV so that they can retain market share. **But how many people recognize that this same graph represents the natural course of their personal relationships?**

If businessmen can recognize when they need to make changes in their business practices so that their companies can continue to grow, **how is it then that these same businessmen are unable to recognize when their personal relationships are failing** and to take the necessary steps to prevent the demise of their relationships.

When I showed this diagram to my young son Justin, he was able to recognize that this is the process that Nintendo incorporated to come up with the Game Cube. He stated that at the point when Nintendo recognized that Sony was targeting the adult market, that Nintendo needed **to be reborn** and that was when they developed the Game Cube.

If you belong to the successful Sony Corporation, how is your personal relationship doing? And if you as an individual are in a loving growing relationship at home, can you explain why your career is in the dumps and why is it that you feel frustration in your individual life, career or within your organization?

The answer lies in our inability to grasp the concept of the need for meaningful change and the inability to be able to implement this type of change into our lives.

The secret to being able to lead a fruitful and productive life lies in the ability to recognize at which point on the graph you as an individual or your organization or relationship or business, currently lie.

If the graph in figure 1 represents the natural course of evolution of change, how then can we prevent ourselves from going down the path represented by phase (D), or decline?

Most of us have heard the phrase, **'it's never too late to change.'** But is this really true, if, as the graph shows, the natural progress in the evolution of change is to follow the downward slope of phase (D)? My answer to this question is a resounding, "Yes!" And I will show by examples both in graphic form and through the use of anecdotes what I mean.

In the words of **my all knowing and all wise son** (he thinks I am dumb), **we need to be reborn,** just like the Nintendo company when its future was threatened by competition from Sony. As I write this paragraph, I can now better understood the following

38

verse from a hymn that I sang in church when I was a child:

"A ruler once came to Jesus at night
And asked him the way to salvation and light.
The Master gave answer in words clear and true,
Ye must be born again."

I now realize that the writer of this verse was not referring to a physical rebirth but to a **spiritual rebirth**. In the same way that we as individuals can experience spiritual rebirth, so too can our businesses and organizations and our society. This is what I meant when I said in an earlier chapter that our physical model will inevitably decline, decay and die but **our mental model can continue to grow indefinitely. Meaningful change is about rebirth.**

Deanna Beisser who wrote a beautiful inspirational book on change and writes some very inspirational poetry, has as the title of one of her books, **'Is it time to change?'**

My answer to the question is, **"Definitely!" It is always time to change. Change (meaningful change)** <u>must</u> **occur for growth to happen. The graph in Figure 1 clearly shows that.**

Meaningful change results in improvement. And as Tiger Woods said in his book **'How I play golf', there is always room for improvement**. If the great Tiger Woods is able to recognize and accept that truth, then I suggest that every one of us had better believe that it is true and to constantly seek for the change that would allow us to continue to grow and develop.

As for the often-asked question, **"Isn't it too late to change?"** my blunt answer is that, **"It is never too late to change!"** I have used this same graph to illustrate this point, in the same manner, as I will also use it in examples of real-life situations to illustrate other aspects of change.

The Story of Jack and Dianne

This is the story of Jack and Dianne,
Two American kids growing up in the heartland.

Dianne (pseudonym) is the name of the patient that I will use to illustrate how and why change is necessary for growth of a relationship. Actually, she and her husband were no longer kids, since they had kids of their own.

Dianne came to see me because she was concerned about her sex life and was bothered by the fact that she and her husband were no longer able to enjoy a satisfying sexual relationship. This was putting a terrible strain on her and it was really affecting her relationship with her husband.

She swore that she loved her husband and he reciprocated the feeling. They were really one of my nicest couples. She wondered if something was seriously wrong with her physically or whether she was going through menopause or whether some of her medications were affecting her. The natural inclination would have been to assume that maybe she was near menopause since she was in her mid-forties.

I knew how much she loved her husband Jack (pseudonym) and it bothered me to see a wonderful (on the surface) relationship going down the drain. I knew instantly that this loving couple needed to see that some meaningful change was necessary to allow their relationship to grow or else they were heading downhill faster than a runaway train without a conductor.

So I invited Dianne to return with her husband Jack for me to attempt to help them.

Why was I, a family physician venturing into the field of marriage counseling? Well, for one thing, Dianne had already gone to several counselors and she had received no help whatsoever. In fact, the counselors had referred her back to me for, **"Guess what?" Anti-depressant pills of course!**

She was in to see me because the counselor had suggested that she was depressed and needed to get medication for her depression. **She** was reluctant to go on anti-depressant medication, **rightfully so**, and **I** was more concerned with addressing the **cause** of her depression rather than simply treating her symptoms.

She and Jack returned to see me and of course, Jack did not see that there was anything for Dianne to bother about. **(Typical macho man!) Jack really was a wonderful guy.** But when I told him that there were major problems in the marriage, his answer was, *"Doc, I love this woman with all my heart. I love her to death and I have told her that there is nothing to worry about."* **Nevertheless, I offered to help them, even though they both professed their love for each other and didn't see how I could help them.**

I produced a diagram of the evolution of change and went through the process. I asked them to identify what stage on the graph they perceived themselves to be and lo and behold, **they instantly recognized that they were in fact on the downhill slope of the graph** and suddenly they were rudely awakened to the fact that they were heading towards separation and possibly divorce. This was a rude shock to them both since they had both professed their love for each other.

The realization of where their marriage was heading made them more willing to participate in the experiment that I was going to embark on with them.

I invited them both to stand in front of my "magical" mirror and asked them both to visualize the image of their relationship as it currently stood. I could see the pained look in Dianne's face and there was a puzzled look on Jack's face and immediately I knew that I was getting my message across.

I then asked them to both look over their **right** shoulder at an image of themselves in the mirror, ten years into the future, **as they would like to see themselves**. When they looked at the image that they had projected, Jack instinctively put his arm around Dianne's shoulders and Dianne developed a smile on her face.

I asked them if they both liked what they saw in the mirror and they both agreed wholeheartedly. I then asked them to look over their **left** shoulder in the mirror and to project the image of themselves **if no change occurred in their relationship**.

At this point, a pained look came over Jack's face and he squeezed Dianne's shoulder tighter. Fear presented itself in Dianne's face and tears welled up in her eyes. Clearly this was not the image that either of them wanted and they said as much when I questioned them.

I then suggested to them that since they both wanted to pursue the path of the image in the right side of the picture, that they needed to come up with meaningful change in their relationship and they needed to formulate a plan and to follow that plan.

They both agreed that they needed to make meaningful change in their relationship but Dianne was still puzzled and said as much. I hastened to inform her that **change did not mean changing partners** but meant that **they both had to change their mental approach to the relationship.**

In other words, they both had to examine the relationship and to come up with ideas of where improvements were needed and how they were going to go about seeking improvements. My mirror does not offer solutions to people's problems. It simply shows people what types of changes are necessary to take them on the path into their future. It is the responsibility of the individual(s) looking into the mirror to come up with appropriate solutions to their problems.

The most dramatic thing that my mirror shows is the consequences if no meaningful change is made, whether that is in them as individuals, in their personal relationships, their careers, their businesses or organizations or in the society.

I have never been as happy as I was when I saw the relief in Dianne's face. The expression in her face showed that she had regained hope after all her fears and anxiety that her marriage could be preserved and grow to levels that she and her husband had never imagined. Jack was equally happy and thanked me profusely. This coming from a man who when he entered my office, was of the opinion that there was nothing wrong with his marriage.

It is at times like these that no amount of money in the world can give me as much satisfaction as the joy I feel when I see the satisfaction in people's eyes after I have helped them. These are huggable moments.

Quite some time later, I received a card from this wonderful couple thanking me for helping them. **I don't need cards. The satisfaction on the patients' faces when they leave my office is more than enough thanks.**

And this is the source of my inspiration to continue writing this book. These people and others will need reinforcement and a source of reference when I am not conveniently available.

My suggestion to everyone who reads this book is to look at the diagrams of the evolution of change and determine at what point on the graph you or your organization are located and figure out where you wish to go from there. In other words, **invent your own future and do not deviate from the path. Follow your dreams and dream as big as you want**. Meaningful change will allow you to accomplish your dreams.

I have included some diagrams of some of our organizations to show examples of what I am referring to throughout the course of this book.

But remember this, no matter where you or your organization are on the evolutionary path of change, you will always benefit from meaningful change.

Where are you and your organization on the Evolutionary path of change?

You need to identify where on the evolutionary path of change you or your organization lies and to figure out what you need to do to make improvements. For instance, if you are at point (A), then you are growing and just need to continue doing what is working for you. If you are at point (B), you are peaking and need to start thinking of innovations. At point (C) change is definitely needed since you are going flat. At point (D) you are going downhill fast and major changes are now necessary. At point (E) you are basically finished and a complete rebirth is necessary at this stage. But note that <u>at any stage on the curve</u>, it is possible to improve the slope of the curve, meaning improved growth (as shown by the dotted lines). The other point to learn is that at any stage, even at (E) change is possible. <u>It is never too late to change!</u>

Figure 1

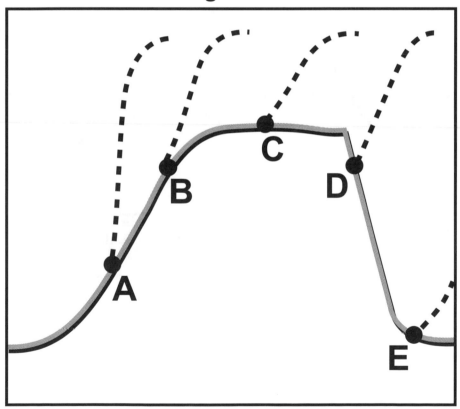

Where on the evolutionary path of change is your
Organization/Career/Relationship?

Figure 2 could possibly represent Microsoft's position on the evolutionary path of change. Microsoft has been one of the most successful companies and continues to develop innovative technologies and so they continue to grow. But as the graph clearly depicts, even Microsoft can go flat and unless they continue to innovate they will go into decline.

Figure 2

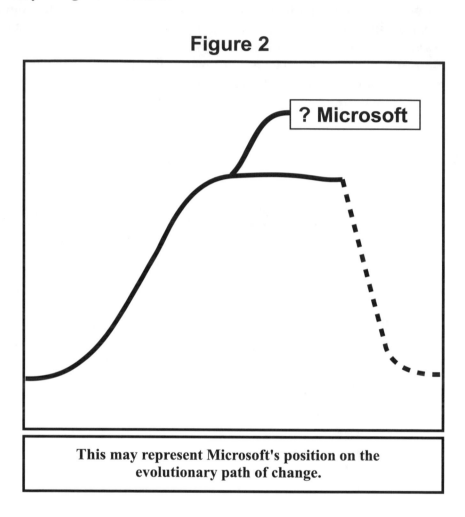

This may represent Microsoft's position on the evolutionary path of change.

This graphic shows the position of two professional football teams relative to each other on the evolutionary path of change. Of note is that the Dallas Cowboys has won several Super Bowl games. The Detroit Lions on the other hand have never got past the first round of the playoffs in recent years. The graph shows that the Detroit Lions have so far failed to get anywhere near their full potential while the Dallas Cowboys are reconstructing themselves after their years of success. Place your own group at whatever point on the chart you belong and work from there to grow.

Figure 3

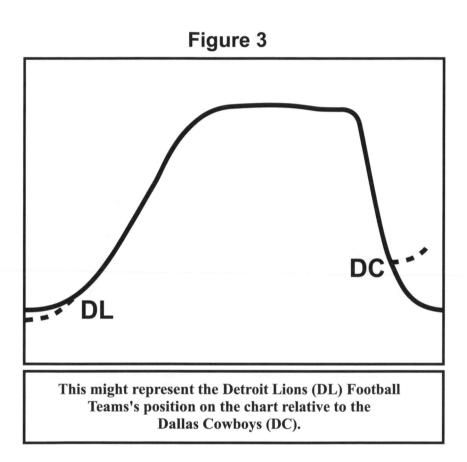

This might represent the Detroit Lions (DL) Football Teams's position on the chart relative to the Dallas Cowboys (DC).

If you find yourself at this stage in your career (A), you need to seriously examine yourself and seek meaningful change in your future. This does not necessarily mean that you have to change jobs but if you don't make some meaningful changes, your job satisfaction is going to go downhill quickly. You have to seek growth to the stage represented by the dotted line(B).

Figure 4

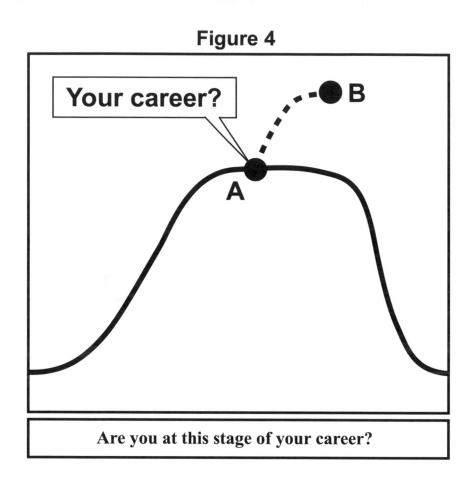

Are you at this stage of your career?

Figure 5 represents the stage on the evolutionary path of change that my patients Jack and Dianne found themselves in their relationship. This could be you in your relationship, in which case as you can see from the graph, your relationship can experience regrowth (dotted lines) and be stronger than it ever was before. This same graphic can represent the United States before and after September 11th. Before September 11th, the US society was in a state of decline. We have the opportunity to become greater than we ever were as a society but we need meaningful change for this to happen.

Figure 5

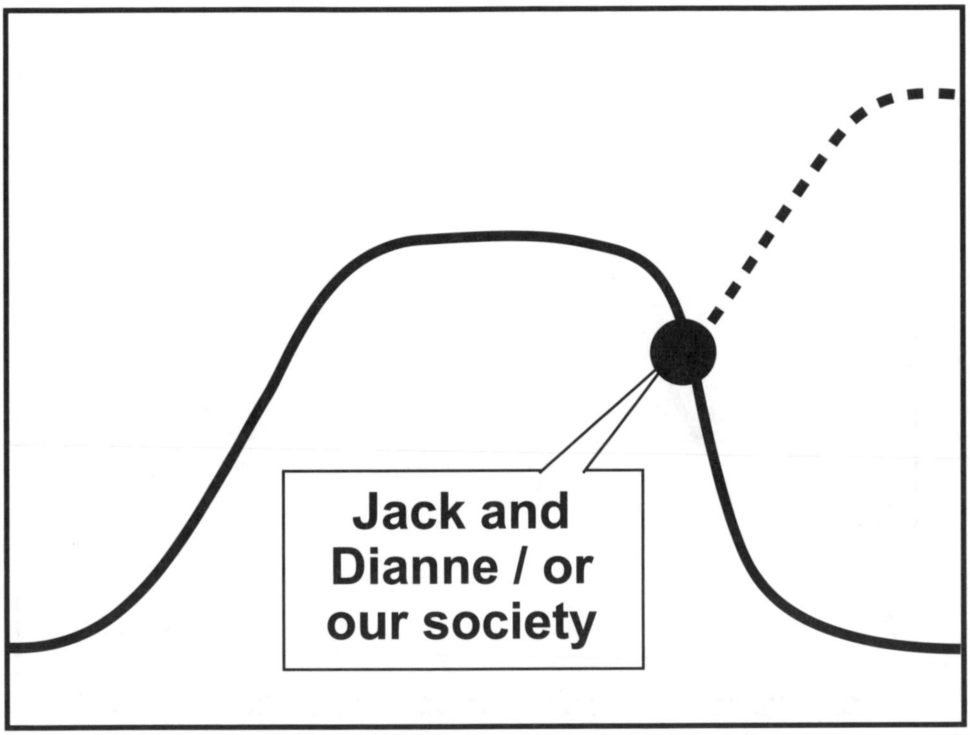

Jack and Dianne / or our society

Jack and Dianne's relationship/or the United States before and after September 11th.

Point A represents the low point in a relationship, career, institution or business. As the diagram shows, meaningful change can result in rebirth of a relationship or career or business etc, and the potential exists for taking the relationship etc. to a level that could exceed the heights previously reached. Such a situation requires willingness on the part of all concerned. Showing the economic benefits can sometimes sway the decision to seek meaningful change. This is what happens when people renew previously failed relationships.

Figure 6

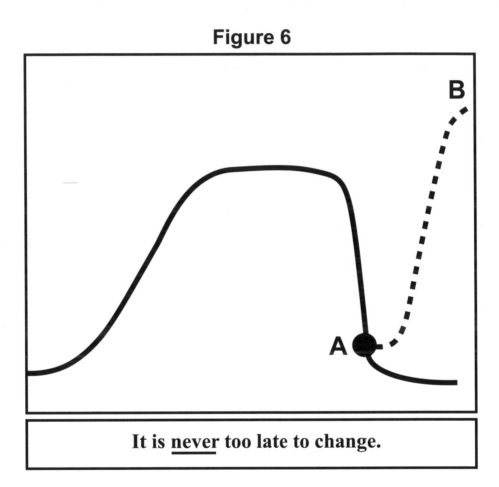

It is <u>never</u> too late to change.

This is why Tiger Woods is the best golfer in the world today. This is also why Michael Jordan was the best basketball player in the world. This is also why John Elway was able to return many years after he had played on 4 losing Super-Bowl teams to win two consecutive Super-Bowl titles. Other players would have quit.

This is also why IBM has stayed at the forefront of technology. There is more to meaningful change than just being competitive. Our very existence requires constant growth and this is only possible through meaningful change.

Figure 7

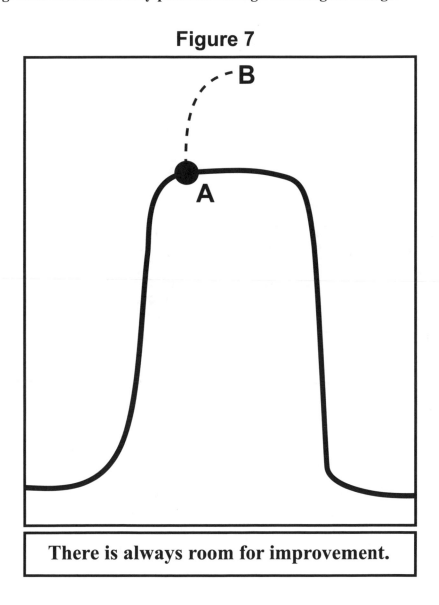

There is always room for improvement.

CHAPTER 4

The Power Of Change

Change your thoughts and you can change the world.

What is change?

Change is a **PROCESS** whereby a **transformation** occurs. When change occurs, something or someone is transformed from one state of being to another. The process can occur in one of several ways. This process can be physical, chemical, mental or any other means by which the transformation occurs.

Electric power can be used to generate electricity, which is transformed into light. The mechanical power of horses was used in the old days to turn water wheels to generate electric power. Solar power is used to generate heat, which in turn is used to run washing machines and refrigerators. The power is harnessed from one source and transformed into power of another form.

The power of change lies in the ability of each and every one of us to change our self and to influence meaningful change in others. That power is greater than any other source of power that exists today, including power generated from the sun.

One individual, of insignificant and humble means, has as much power as any other individual to change the entire course of our world. I will use an analogy to illustrate this point in a subsequent section of the book when dealing with, 'our world and the need for change.'

Suffice it to say that our whole world was changed by the teachings of a humble carpenter's son, who was Himself a humble fisherman.

Mahatma Gandhi changed the course of the entire Indian sub-continent by his ability to influence meaningful change in others. The same applies to Martin Luther King Jr. who helped change the course of American history. History abounds with individuals of humble upbringing who through their ability to influence meaningful change were able to change the entire course of world history.

So you say that you are not Mahatma Gandhi or Martin Luther King Jr. and you

certainly are not Jesus Christ, although you have used his name often enough when things were not going your way. *But the awesome power of change exists because of our inter-connectedness with the rest of the universe. Change in one individual is transformed into change in other individuals and spreads exponentially to affect every other individual in the world*. This point is very well demonstrated in the chapter, **'Our World and the Need for Change.'**

The Mental Model

Within each and every one of us exists that awesome power to change us and to influence meaningful change **in others**. The challenge comes from learning how to harness that power and to be able to use it effectively. This is the **'Power to be able to influence change.'**

Every individual, every relationship, every company, organization, society and community, exists within a physical model and operates through a mental model. The physical model is the structure that is visible to the naked eye.

The mental model represents the core values of the individual, the relationship, the company, the institution, the organization, the community or the society. It is much easier to grasp the concept of the physical model than that of the mental model.

In order to understand the process of change, it is vital that we get a good grasp of the concept of what is meant by one's mental model. I will continue to provide examples of this concept throughout the book. Understanding the concept of one's mental model is fundamental to understanding the process of change.

It is a natural process of life and a fact of life that the <u>physical being</u> will ultimately decay and die. Every individual, every organization, every society, every relationship, will undergo a process whereby the **<u>physical structure</u>** will ultimately decay and die.

The physical model will inevitably go into a state of decline, decay and eventually death. Every building will naturally decay and will likely undergo demolition or crumble on its own, unless constant remodeling occurs.

Mental models on the other hand have the capacity for unlimited growth. But for growth to occur, change has to constantly occur. As individuals and in our organizations, when our mental models cease to change, decline and decay sets in and the organism or the organization is effectively dead and we become just like the title of the movie, **'Dead Man Walking.'**

It is through meaningful change in our mental model that we are able to effect meaningful change in our physical model. The reverse does not necessarily hold true. So we see that changing the mental model is all-important for growth and

development of the organism or organization.

Take a look around and try to identify the walking zombies among us, in our organizations and in our societies. These are individuals, relationships, businesses and organizations that are occupying space but have not made any type of meaningful change in ages. In other words, they are effectively dead. Just like the proverbial rotten apple in the barrel, these individuals or organizations can poison entire systems.

Individuals, relationships, businesses, companies and organizations all grow through growth of the mental models. The physical model or physical plant will decay and may die. **That is a fundamental law of nature**. The mental model on the contrary has the capacity for infinite growth. **When Jesus Christ died, his physical body was interred. But His mental model survives in the world today and continues to grow. That is the power of change.**

When individuals or relationships or businesses or organizations or entire societies fail, it is as a direct result of failure of individuals or organizations to change their mental models.

How often have we not heard of individuals who were taken away by undertakers because they were presumed dead only to be recognized later to actually be living? Such individuals often awake with the same degree of shock as the undertakers when each party realizes what has happened.

My advice to every individual in any relationship or any business or organization is to wake up and show some movement, show some change; before you are shocked by the realization that you were discarded because someone presumed that you were dead! Do not appear stagnant. Make some type of meaningful change or you too will be presumed dead and will be carted away.

Open up your mind and let the sun shine in.

The only means of strengthening one's intellect is to make up one's mind about nothing- to let the mind be a thoroughfare for all thoughts.
John Keats

Change can **appear** to occur incidentally or co-incidentally or it can occur as a result of a conscious process. **Meaningful change only occurs when there is a change of the mental model of the individual, relationship, organization, society or spiritual being.**

As previously stated, each of us exists within a mental model and a physical model. Our mental models are defined by the assumptions that we foster in our thought processes. If we were to look into a mirror, we would see a physical image of our self. This is our physical model. **We cannot visualize our mental model in a mirror.**

Our mental model is represented by our conscience and our values and the assumptions we hold. As I have stated earlier in another section of the book, assumptions are self-limiting and are likely to be proven false ultimately.

I understood this statement better when my good friend and colleague Dr Hugh Holder reminded me, that at his commencement address during graduation from medical school, the keynote speaker told the graduating class, **"Fifty percent of what you have been taught in medical school today would eventually be proven to be false! The problem is that no one knows which fifty percent it would be."**

By my own extrapolation, I deduced that since no one knew which fifty percent of what we were taught in medical school was false, then the possibility existed that EVERYTHING we learnt in medical school was likely to be false. However when we entered medical school, our assumption was that everything that the professors taught us was true.

Assumptions are self-limiting and are usually false. Until Galileo proved otherwise, every scientist of the period assumed that the world was flat. How often have we not assumed something to be true, only to be shocked when we discover the truth? **Get rid of your fixed assumptions before you can even hope to make meaningful change.**

In this book and in my life, I have adopted a Galilean attitude. I encourage all those who seek to effect meaningful change to think like Galileo.

When I suggest that we need to change our mental model, I am suggesting that we need to eliminate every fixed assumption we have ever held about anything and about everything.

As I stated earlier it is much easier to understand the concept of the physical model than the mental model. The physical model is what is visible externally to others. When we look at an individual or a company or a society, we can easily visualize the physical forms. What is harder to visualize is the mental model of the individual or the company or the society or the institution. *We cannot judge the contents of a book by looking at its cover. We all know this and we have been told it repeatedly. But how many of us operate outside of this model?*

'I was at a New Year's Eve party in Canada recently. I stayed at a Holiday Inn hotel where a gala New Year's Eve celebration was planned. Since I was only in Canada visiting relatives, I hadn't made plans to attend any type of New Year's Eve parties and so I didn't walk with any formal wear. However I did take a very nice sweater and a pair of dress pants.

Being a guest at the hotel, I decided on the spur of the moment to attend the reception and I invited some friends to join us for the evening. All the males were elegantly dressed in suits, except me of course. But being the poster boy of meaningful change that I have become, I wore my very nice sweater and thought that I looked very nice.

In fact, as the evening progressed and every one became hot and sweaty from all the dancing and wine, many of the men were forced to remove their jackets. I felt pretty smug about my decision to wear a sweater and felt very good about my decision to do so.

My wife however did not have the same opinion, as most wives do and she didn't hesitate to tell me how much I stood out from the other men at the party. She looked at a gentleman of Asian extraction and commented 'how elegant the Filipino doctor looked in his suit. We have several friends who are Filipino and who are doctors and carry themselves in a very distinguished manner. But I also know that all Filipino doctors do not have the same physical attributes and also that all Filipinos who wear suits and carry themselves elegantly are not doctors.

When I asked my wife how she knew that the gentleman in question was (a) Filipino and (b) that he was a doctor, she insisted that she just knew and instructed me to hold any further opinions that I had about the very nicely dressed gentleman to myself. She was very polite but forceful about it and I knew well enough to shut my mouth.

The next day while on our way home by car, we heard a beautiful song by a female artiste that neither my wife nor I seemed to have heard before. I asked my wife who she thought the singer might be. She mentioned the name of a white singer and I was inclined to go along with who she thought it might be.

My son who had appeared to be sleeping in the back seat chimed in, "No mom, that's Janet Jackson." I of course had to open my big mouth and restart the discussion about the "Filipino' gentleman at the party and how we should not judge people by their appearance. Needless to say, my dinner that evening consisted of a Burger King hamburger. I should learn to keep my big mouth shut at the appropriate times.'

When we look at a GM plant or a hospital or a Mc Donald's restaurant, we can see their physical model in the same way that we can see an individual's. **What we cannot see are the mental models that lie within the physical structures**. But what if a blind person was looking at the same structures? What would such a person see?

The mental model is represented by the *values* of the individual, the company, the organization, the society and our world. The blind person is able to visualize the mental model of an individual or a company or an institution or even society much easier than the sighted person.

In order to visualize what the mental model of an individual or an organization represents, we must begin to look at things like a sightless person would.

Changing the mental model is a fundamental concept when we attempt to motivate others to make behavioral changes, whether they need to lose weight, quit smoking, handle their anxiety and depression or to better manage their disease states or to develop their personal relationships or grow their businesses or their organization.

The same concept must be applied when we seek to encourage others to become more community oriented, or when businesses or organizations pursue growth.

For example, if we wish to encourage neighbors, who allow their surroundings to deteriorate, to maintain clean and beautiful surroundings (the physical model), we must first show them why it would benefit them to think of doing so (change their mental model).

Meaningful changes are made only when we change our mental models. We can change our physical model and yet retain the same mental model. A leopard can change its spots but it would still be a leopard and it would still do leopard things (like attacking you.) That is not meaningful change. When the mental model changes however, then meaningful change does occur. Osama Bin Laden with a clean shaved face and dressed in western suits will still be the same person. The problem with most books on change is they do not seek to differentiate between meaningful changes and change per se. This is why the majority of people who have read those books have not benefited.

The movie "Face Off", in which John Travolta and Nicholas Cage starred, aptly demonstrates the concept of the physical model and the mental model beautifully.

In this movie, the villain (Nicholas Cage) plots to take over the physical features of the hero (JohnTravolta) by surreptitiously arranging for and succeeding with a transplant of each other's face. Despite successfully accomplishing the physical change, each individual retains his own personality and the villain ultimately is exposed and destroyed because he is unable to conceal his evil ways.

Cosmetic changes are not meaningful changes. What we need in our lives are meaningful changes and that only comes from changing the mental model.

This same principle is as equally applicable to individuals as it is to relationships, businesses, companies, organizations and institutions, or society. I cannot emphasize this point often enough. It is nothing short of remarkable how many people see the process of change as being different when comparing their individual lives with their relationships or businesses.

A company, organization or institution may change its physical plant i.e. its physical model and yet fail to change its mental model.

It is the core values of the company or organization that are reflected in its men-

tal model. If the core values (the mental model) of a company or organization remain the same, no amount of change in the physical plant will improve the success of that company or organization. **Meaningful change occurs only when an individual, company, organization or society changes its mental model**.

No matter what type of facility the Klu Klux Klan operate from, or whether or not they wear sheets or suits, their mental model remains the same. The same applies to the Black Panthers or Muslim fundamentalists or members of any other group that operates with fixed assumptions within closed mental models.

When the Taliban were routed in Afghanistan, many of their members shaved their beards to conceal their identity. The fact remains that these people still retain their retarded and regressive beliefs about the way the country should be run and how others should run their lives. Any one who believes that these individuals have changed is likely to be rudely shocked when these individuals revert to their old ways.

In the aftermath of September 11th, when I was crossing the Canadian border, my family and friends encouraged me to shave my beard, lest I would be mistaken for a terrorist. My reply was that if a beard was the identifying feature of terrorists, then it is possible that the father of terrorism himself, good old Abraham Lincoln, probably ran this country.

I am pleased to say that at no time while crossing the border was I stopped because of my beard. That is another example of meaningful change; when we cease to stereotype others.

Recently, Philip Morris announced a decision to change its name. I am not certain of the reason for this but I can only presume that it was done to improve the corporate image that has in recent times taken a battering because of the products Philip Morris manufactures.

The fact remains that Philip Morris or whatever its new name, continues to manufacture and distribute a product which is detrimental to society's well being. Philip Morris has changed its physical model (it's name) but its mental model remains the same (selling a harmful product).

Meaningful change will occur only when Philip Morris changes its' core values and ceases to manufacture products that are harmful to society.

I have used Philip Morris as an example of how the physical and mental model works. The same principle can be extrapolated to any other company, organization or even to our society.

When we understand this concept of changing the mental model, we are then able to understand why racism bigotry and discrimination still exist and persist in our society, even to this day, in spite of all the books on change that are currently in publication.

When we as physicians treat our patients, what we are hoping to achieve is that these patients will change their mental model of how they perceive their health so that they can take control and responsibility for their own health. Changing their mental models would empower them and influence them to visualize and implement changes in their physical models (their health).

It is only through a change in the mental model of our patients that we as physicians will be most likely able to effect meaningful changes in them. Unless we could get our patients to change their mental model, the results of our interventions are short term and meaningless.

This is the fundamental problem with healthcare **throughout the world** today. **This is why the health care systems of Britain, Canada, the USA and most other countries are facing the crisis that they are in today and unless physicians and patients make meaningful change, we will continue on the path of self-destruction. And we will have no one else but ourselves to blame.**

Meaningful change then, comes about when we are able to teach others how to change their mental model. But how are we going to be able to do this?

There are six essential steps involved in the **"Process of Change"**. These steps are:

1. Recognition of the need to change.
2. Visualization of the desired results of change and <u>the consequence of no change</u>.
3. Acceptance of the need to change
4. Desire to change
5. Planning a mental map for change.
6. Implementation of the plan to change (following the map).

Change is a cyclical process and for it to be meaningful, it has to be an ongoing process: see diagram (Figure 9):

The old man and the sea

How many times in your life have you not wished and longed for the simple times and wished to get back to **the good old days? Would you really?**

Very few people recognize the need for change or are willing to change spontaneously. While writing this book, I remembered the following anecdote that a friend of a friend told me.

'One fine day on the beautiful island of Trinidad and Tobago, a tourist happened

to encounter an old man pulling up his glass-bottomed boat onto the shore. The older man used his boat for taking tourists out to sea and used it for catching fish when business was slow.

The old man lived in a little shack by the beach and basically lived a simple, contented life. He had never left the island of Trinidad and Tobago. (I could never understand why two islands are referred to as the ISLAND of Trinidad and Tobago.) But they have their own quirks there. This is an island where everything shuts down for one week so that the whole country can celebrate Carnival.

Anyway, the two of them exchange cordial greetings and the conversation proceeds like this:'

Old Guy: *"Howdy? Where you come from man?"*

Tourist: *"I am from the United States."*

Old Guy: *"No, no! I mean where you were born."*

Tourist: *"Oh! I was born right here in Trinidad and Tobago."*

Old Guy: *"Me see! So what is your name?"*

Tourist: *" My name is Harry Mendoza. And what is your name sir?"*

Old Guy: *" Me name Babulall Bailam Singh!" So you from America eh? You must got a lotta money eh? You got a big job eh?"*

Tourist: *"Certainly! I have done pretty well for myself. I have a pretty decent job and I earn a decent living. In fact I own my own company!*

Old Guy: *" Eh! Eh! That good man! That real good! So tell me, you mussee had to study hard fuh that eh?"*

Tourist: *"You're right. I first studied in England, then I went to Canada and did some further studies and then I completed my PhD in the U.S".*

Old Guy (in genuine amazement): *"Wow! That musta been hard eh man? How long that take for you to do?"*

Tourist: *"Oh, it was tough alright. It took me a total of fifteen years!"*

Old Guy (mouth agape in even more astonishment): *"Fifteen years! Fifteen years? Man, that musta been real tough. You deserve all the money you got. So now you on holiday, eh?"*

Tourist: *"Yes sir. I really needed a break. In fact, I am thinking of retiring soon."*

Old Guy (in shock): *"Retire! Retire? Man, when you can make all that money you will retire now? What you plan to do when you retire?"*

Tourist: *"Oh! Actually I was thinking of returning home here to Trinidad and Tobago."*

Old Guy (surprised again): *"Come back here!? And then what you plan to do?"*

Tourist: *"Oh. I think I would like to buy a little boat, get a little house on the beach, do some fishing and just relax."*

The old man developed a puzzled look on his face, pondered and then he proceeded, *"But wait man, isn't that what I have been doing all my life? Tell me Harry, why you fellas always like to take the long way around?"*

This anecdote amply explains why some of us change and some do not. We all need change in our lives for growth and development. But some of us **choose** not to and some of us simply see no reason to do so. But relationships, businesses, organizations and societies **must** change for growth to occur.

Many individuals are content to continue their daily "humdrum lives" and are content with a basic existence. That is fine as long as we recognize that such situations will not result in growth and the real possibility of decline and decay exists.

Unlike the old man, I still prefer to continue to explore new avenues for growth. After all, just like the old man, I too once lived on the beach in the beautiful island of Barbados. But I became bored out of my skull with my lack of mental growth. I felt like Kermit the frog, sitting on a large rock in the middle of the Caribbean Sea and so I moved to cold, snowy, damp, overcast Michigan.

Call me crazy if you like but I appreciate the sunshine better after I have experienced months of rain (and snow). For me there is nothing more beautiful and there is no better feeling in the world than seeing that first tulip coming out of the ground, announcing the start of spring, after a long cold winter.

I remember how exhilarating it felt, feeling the first cold, chilly autumn breeze in my face and watching the first falling leaf fluttering and circling like a dancing fairy before settling gently on the ground. And I felt sorry for my friends in Barbados and other parts of the world where the seasons never change and who could never experience such a beautiful feeling.

That old man may have been content to live within his insular world but I am certain that he could not appreciate the beauty of the beach or his surroundings in the same degree as Harry the tourist who had missed those things for so long.

Through an understanding of the process of change and an understanding of how to apply these concepts in our daily lives, we can by changing our mental model help others to change **their** mental model and through understanding the principle of **interconnectedness**, we are able to understand how, by changing our thoughts we can succeed in changing the world.

All change sets in motion a chain of other reactions that affect events and people in every corner of the globe.

When we throw a stone into a pond, the ripples spread out to every corner of the pond. To the student of physics, we know that when we throw a rock into a river, the energy spreads to every tributary of that river and ultimately to the far ends of the earth. **So too with change!**

Change in one individual sets up a chain reaction which ultimately affects others at the far corners of the globe. But as any student of physics would understand, the energy of the reaction comes right back to us. This is the cycle of change.

'He who sows the wind will reap the whirlwind. He who sows the seeds of meaningful change will reap rich bounties and spiritual wealth'.

In order to comprehend how change in one individual affects every one else, we need to get a grasp of the principle of inter-connectedness. This concept is embodied in what is known as **'General Systems Theory'**. This theory suggests that **we are all part of an organization of systems in the same way that the human body is made up of a number of inter-related systems**.

Defects or failure of one system or one part of a system negatively affects all other systems. All systems must be operating optimally for the organism (organization) to function optimally.

Whether we have a headache or constipation, our entire functional status is affected. This is a crude but simple to understand analogy that shows that every system has an equally important role in the effective function of the whole organism or organization.

Understanding this very basic concept of inter-connectedness, helps us to understand the importance of the lowest member of any organization. *Understanding the concept of inter -connectedness helps us to understand why the plight of people starving in Africa and suffering from the devastation of AIDS is our problem also.*

Let's take an example of the following hypothetical situation:

'Suppose that you belong to a large organization that is seeking to do business with a very wealthy and influential client. You and your entire organization have done your utmost to ensure that everything is done to accommodate your client and to enhance the visit. The client is greeted at the entrance of your facility by the valet who parks the client's car. You lay out the red carpet and take the client to the finest restaurant. You lay out your company policy and business proposition to the client.

Everything goes like clockwork and both you and the client are extremely satisfied. The deal is likely to be finalized as soon as the client returns home and discusses the matter with his board of directors.

The service that is provided from the time the client arrives is excellent. Yet when the client is about to leave, the parking attendant is extremely rude or unhelpful. Worse yet, the client discovers that while she was in the meeting, the valet decided to take her three hundred and fifty thousand dollars Lamborghini for a joy ride and even worse, crashes the vehicle. This final experience, by probably the lowliest member of your organization can quite conceivably affect the entire future of your company.

I have had such an experience at a Ritz Carlton hotel. The Ritz Carlton is reputed to be one of the finest run organizations and is often referred to at business seminars as to how a corporation should be run. I have heard this statement repeated over and over again and I have heard colleagues stating that the Ritz should be used as an example of how an efficient business should be run.

Yet, this runs counter with my personal experience with the Ritz. On my first visit to a Ritz Carlton hotel, before I had registered at the reception desk, the valet and the bellboys dressed in their top hats and wearing white gloves 'a la Michael Jackson style' greeted me. Of course I was suitably impressed and my wife and I looked forward to a fantastic weekend.

But in this very swank hotel, the receptionist at the front desk must have had a bad day at home or at work. She was extremely rude and very unhelpful. To compound matters, we were told that our room, which had been reserved prior to our arrival, was not ready. My wife and several other spouses of other doctors were made to wait in the lobby of the hotel for approximately three hours while I attended my conference.

Even after I was finished with my conference, three hours later, our room was still not ready. No one made an effort to offer the guests who were sitting in the lobby any other suitable type of accommodation while they were waiting for their spouses.

To compound matters, when we were finally assigned to a room, we found the view overlooking a parking garage or some other such hideous building. Even worse yet, my allergies bothered me all night because the pillows in the room were feather pillows, to which I am severely allergic.

When I attempted to voice my displeasure the following morning, the receptionist, who was probably still having another bad day at home or at work simply shrugged me off. Needless to say, this was an extremely unpleasant experience

This was my first experience of the Ritz but it left such a bad tasting experience in my mouth that because of that first experience. I have never returned to a Ritz Carlton hotel, even after the General Manager offered me a free weekend at one of their hotels for my wife and me, to compensate for our bad experience, after I wrote a letter of complaint.

As the general manager explained in his letter of apology, "We would like you to return so that we can show you what Ritz service is really like." **Really?** So what was my first experience all about then? How would I know that they were not putting on a special act for me to try to compensate for my poor experience? The point here is to show how sometimes, an employee at the bottom of the food chain can adversely affect the success of a major organization.

I do not doubt that the Ritz Carlton is a fine organization but I prefer to stay at Holiday Inns where I am a Priority Club member and where I have always been treated like royalty because of my priority club status (which is free incidentally).

As soon as I make my reservation at a Holiday Inn, I am immediately upgraded to a more expensive room with no increase in cost. My breakfast is included in the cost of the room and several other perks are included. The rooms that I am assigned are at least as good as any in the fanciest of hotels at which I have stayed and if anything is sometimes usually better.

Can you picture a poor country boy like me living the life of Riley?

But best of all, I usually end up paying about one third the price that the so-called luxury hotels charge, invariably for their gaudy and ostentatious lobbies.

I am not sure how many people sleep in hotel lobbies but my own experience of hotel lobbies is generally when I am checking in or when I am trying to sneak out so that I can avoid tipping the bellboys. The truth is, I can usually find lots more interesting things to do than spend my time in hotel lobbies. *By this stage in my life, I am familiar with what constitutes meaningful change and I am capable of making the discrimination between pomp and show and meaningful change when I see it.*

Another aspect of change that needs to be considered and is often ignored is the wide-ranging effect that change can have. This is **the ripple effect of change**. **No action stands by itself without causing a chain of other reactions. We understand this from the ripple effect when we throw a pebble in a pond. I will discuss this again in another section of the book.**

I recall another incident that occurred in my experience that demonstrates this point graphically.

'Prior to the opening of a beautiful new golf course in Michigan, **(I had chanced to discover this course quite by accident)** *I convinced another friend that we should play this course as soon as it was opened. Consequently, within the first week of the opening of the course, we had organized a large group and we sallied forth to play the course.*

The beauty of the course and the hospitality of the staff in that first week enthralled us. As soon as we returned home, we spread the word of this beautiful course to all our friends. Soon, we had organized several other large groups to visit and play this spectacular course, which I must add was not cheap by any means. But we all felt that the beauty of the course justified the cost.

The exposure that the course obtained just from one individual was enormous and word about this course spread faster than if they had received rave reviews in the magazine Golf Digest. Consequently the popularity of the course increased rapidly.

Well, consistent with all that is bad about human behavior and the lack of vision about how to effect meaningful change, the owners of the course believed that they had stumbled upon the goose that laid golden eggs. They believed that they had acquired an asset that was indispensable to all golfers.

They proceeded to raise the green fees from an already high level to a level that was prohibitive. But worse yet, the attitude that the management adopted was such that the official policy appeared to be one of rushing players to complete their rounds so that they could increase the numbers utilizing the course.

No one, and I mean no one, who likes to play golf, no matter how much of a fanatic you are, enjoys being treated poorly on a golf course, especially after you have driven two and a half to three hours to play that course, no matter how beautiful it is. Soon, word spread about the attitude of the management.

I cannot tell you how many large groups have since absolutely refused to visit that course. I must add that Michigan has over one thousand golf courses, many of which are among some of the most beautiful in the world. Golfers in Michigan are not hurting for beautiful golf courses.'

As word spreads however, that particular golf course could find itself hurting from the negative publicity that it has generated among other golfers.

Before we can change or influence others to change, there needs to be a **willingness to embrace change**. In other words, **we must first desire and conceive change before we can make meaningful change happen**. On the other hand we are sometimes forced by circumstances to change.

Crisis often forces change and it is unfortunate that we very often wait until critical situations develop before we elect to change. We are retroactive rather than proactive.

The September 11th tragedy forced us to change many aspects of our lives. We changed our strategy as far as airport security was concerned. We were forced to review and make changes in our internal security. We changed our banking reg-

ulations. We revised the processes whereby terrorists could be tried for their crimes. We reviewed and renewed our spirituality at least temporarily. We changed our entire lifestyles.

It was stated by many that the September 11th tragedy changed us forever. Of course it did! But these were changes we needed to make, even before September 11th.

The reason we did not make these changes is that we could not see the need to change in some situations, we did not care to change in other situations and we did not understand how to effect meaningful change in yet others.

After September 11th our society became united like it had never before been united. For the first time since Pearl Harbor, our politicians and leaders were united and worked together in a common cause, to lead our country into the future.

The people in California were genuinely concerned about the welfare of the people in New York. People dug deeply into their pockets without being asked and donated money, food and services freely.

In one week, over $1.5 billion dollars were collected to help the victims and survivors of that dastardly attack. **Where was this money before?** *If we had asked people to donate the same amount of money to assist the 35 million without health care insurance in this country, would we have got the same response?* I doubt it very much!

The changes that followed September 11th were all necessary changes but it needed a crisis of major proportions to enlighten us. **We waited until a major crisis developed before we *elected* to change**. People who had never before heard of Tajikistan or Uzbekistan were genuinely concerned about the plight of refugees in those countries.

The problem is that when crisis forces us to change, we are generally unprepared for this and this can create fear and doubts and uncertainty. Crisis forces such rapid change that the result is usually turmoil and chaos.

The speed with which we are forced to change as a result of crisis is much greater than when we <u>anticipate</u> the need for change and plan for those changes to occur. *Crisis shocks our system and I do not know of anyone who likes to be shocked.*

But we can avoid these unpleasant experiences if we understand the need for, plan for and learn how to effect meaningful change **before a crisis** develops.

Crisis leads to short term change. **Short-term change is not meaningful change. For meaningful change to occur, we need to change our mental model and teach others how to do the same.**

When people state, with a more than a twinge of regret in their voice, that September 11th changed us forever, the implication is that when September 11th changed us forever that this was regrettable. I disagree completely!

The fact is that prior to September 11th, our society was in a state of decline. Drugs were a bane of our society. Our youth lacked direction. Teenagers were piercing every part of their bodies and tattooing every other part, with the potential risks of spread of hepatitis. Our youth lacked direction. Their lives had no meaning. Pornography was becoming the norm. A white slave trade has replaced the black slave trade where young girls are being enslaved into pornography. School shootings were becoming everyday occurrences. Our society lacked direction. We needed a change of our mental model.

As I have previously stated, change **must** and does need to occur **constantly** for growth and development to occur. What is regrettable is that we wait for crisis in our lives to force us to change.

The difference between changes that are forced upon us by crisis as opposed to planned change is the rapidity with which the former develops. The consequence is that such change is unanticipated, is a shock to our system and is often accompanied by fear and uncertainty. **Who among us would deny that September 11th shocked us to the bone?**

We absolutely need to change our mental model for meaningful and long-lasting change to occur. Furthermore unless we recognize the need to change our mental model, change that is forced upon us by crisis is often only temporary. As soon as the crisis has abated, we revert to our original behaviors.

On the contrary, change that is planned because of a change in our mental model is often longer lasting and more permanent and likely to be more meaningful.

The reason that the Taliban and the Islamic fundamentalists failed and will not flourish in Afghanistan or anywhere else in the world is because they operate within a mental model that has not changed in over two thousand years. The world has changed but they still operate within a mental model that was suitable for the middle ages! The same holds true for other organizations and institutions in our society.

My perception of the effects of September 11th tragedy is that **we have the potential** and the capacity to become the greatest society since the dawn of civilization. What is left for us to see is whether we have changed our mental model. I know that we can change our mental model. The question is, will we?

We have the potential to become and remain a truly united society. We have the potential to become a more tolerant society. We have the potential to eradicate discrimination of all forms and I can see great hope for the future. But for meaningful change to be permanent, **we must change our mental model!**

Crisis not only results in change but often also results in connectedness. People are generally forced to come together in times of crisis as exemplified so vividly by the September 11th tragedy.

Why is it necessary for crisis to occur before we are forced to unite for the common good and come together to change? Is it such a difficult concept to realize that we can make **voluntary decisions to change** to effect a smoother transition?

For us to achieve this effect requires us to become futurists. We need to think in the future and live in the future. I will elaborate on this concept later. *The past is dead and gone. We can use the lessons of the past to help shape our future but we cannot live in the past!*

The doctrine of change states that change is essential for growth and life to continue. The very essence of life is all about change. The need for **meaningful** change is a fundamental law of life.!

This principle is embodied in the very simple product life cycle with which business people are so familiar as seen in the diagram in figure 1. And after all, we are in the business of life.

Picture a pool of water in your backyard. What happens to stagnant water? That stagnant pool begins to attract colonies of bacteria. It becomes polluted and starts to develop a foul odor. Contrast this stagnant pool of water with that of a mountain stream. Because the water is constantly flowing it remains fresh. Bacteria cannot multiply as easily. The mountain stream has a clean fresh smell. The water tastes fresh. It is a joy to swim in that stream.

So too with our daily lives and so too with our organizations and so too with our relationships! **Without change in our daily lives, we suffer mental stagnation**. We become polluted with the bacteria of negative thoughts. We emanate the awful odor of negativity and there is no desire for others to wish to associate with us. In other words we become pools of stagnant water.

On the other hand, consider the individual whose life is constantly refreshed with new ideas and challenges. It is a joy to be in the company of such an individual. Our own lives become enriched purely from association with such individuals. Such individuals are like the clean fresh mountain streams. We all would like to frolic in that stream.

If we as individuals would like to attract others to us and to our ideas, we need to constantly implement new ideas and to foster change.

I constantly stress throughout this book that the same principles of change apply to individuals as they do to businesses, organizations, societies, personal relationships and to our spiritual being.

It is almost like an epiphany when I point out to my patients how to conduct the "mirror experiment" as I have described in another section of this book. This is illustrated in greater detail in the section on how to conduct the "mirror experiment."

In analyzing the process of change, **the question is not whether change is necessary or whether change is possible. These questions should not even arise**. Not only is meaningful change absolutely necessary but it is **also economically sound** as I will show in subsequent chapters. **Meaningful change benefits all of us and it is certainly within the power of each and every one of us**.

The question we should ask is whether the individual or organization **desires** change and **if not, why not?** We will never be able to effect meaningful change in others or us unless the desire to change comes from within. Could we have ever hoped to effect meaningful change in the likes of Jeffery Dahmer or Osama Bin Laden? The answer is yes. The reason we were not able to do so was not because it wasn't possible but because these individuals simply didn't want to change. **Some people just won't change**.

Can you change your mental model? Would you <u>wish</u> to change your mental model? What would be the <u>consequence of not changing your mental model</u> five years or ten years from now? <u>How</u> can you change your mental model? <u>Will</u> you change your mental model? These are the questions that this book addresses.

If we are to prevent stagnation and to foster growth we need to constantly change our mental models and constantly make updates or changes to prevent "bacteriological" overgrowth. The same concept applies in our relationships with others. Why do so many relationships fail? Why are there so many divorces in our society? The answer lies in our inability to effect meaningful changes in our mental models.

Have you ever entered a room that has been closed up for a long period of time. The air inside that room can be stifling and choking. The fresh air that enters that room when you open a window is invigorating. We need to open up the windows to our soul and experience the fresh air outside our windows.

My good friend and golfing buddy **Todd Howhart** understood this and shared this gem with me. (**Poor Todd, it hasn't made any difference to his golf game however**).

I am positive that when Todd reads this he will resolve to take all my money on the golf course the next time we play. Ah well, what the heck!

We continue to foster stagnation in our lives and in our relationships and our organizations. Soon our relationships have such a foul odor that we no longer wish to be swimming in that cesspool of contamination. We then seek out streams of flowing water where we can feel refreshed.

But unless we understand the concept of how to effect meaningful change, those new streams too, soon become polluted. **This is the reason most relationships fail and do so repeatedly; through the inability of one or both parties to see the need or the ability to effect meaningful change.**

No one in his/her right senses wants to stay in a relationship that is not growing. Such relationships develop a stench. **The secret is to keep the relationship growing and flowing.** This comes from making constant and **meaningful** changes.

This is why we also need to keep both our physical and mental models in tune and updated. If either model fails to change, "bacteriological" overgrowth sets in and the stench becomes too overbearing for us to want to stay around (**unless we have some type of co-dependent or demented personality**).

This same concept is no less true of our communities or our organizations, whether these are our workplaces or our institutions. **It was fascinating to see the "passengers" (employees) jump ship when the technology companies stopped growing and went into a rapid state of decline.**

These companies grew and matured extremely quickly and stopped making meaningful changes. Overnight we had a new breed of multi-millionaires who because of their inexperience had no clue what to do about further growth. They lacked understanding of the philosophy of meaningful change. **Consequently their decline was just as rapid as Dolly the cloned sheep that aged and declined so rapidly. The latest report on Dolly is that she has developed arthritis at a relatively young age.** *Silicon Valley too has developed arthritis in all its joints.*

We must realize that change can be positive, or negative. There is no in-between or gray area in change. Once stagnation sets in, unless meaningful change occurs, the next stage is decline and death soon follows. **Negative change comes about purely as a result of doing NOTHING.** The mere act of doing nothing different from our daily-accustomed activities will result in pollution as in the case of the stagnant pool of water.

Positive change on the other hand is a dynamic process. In other words we must want to change and we must seek out change. Water does not flow upwards except if we use a pump. We can **LET change happen** (as when water flows downhill) or we can **MAKE change happen** (as when we use a pump to pump water against gravity). In other words we can invent our future. But before we can invent our future, we must be capable of visualizing the future.

We can picture the future, as we would like it to happen and plan for that future. Or we can let the future jump up on us unanticipated and in which case we become the past. This is what "futurism' is all about. *If we do not anticipate and plan for the future, we will become as extinct as the dinosaurs!*

We need to take a more detailed look at ourselves, as individuals, at our relationships, communities, organizations, society, country and world (including our universe) and our relationship with God. In other words, **we need to take a look at the TOTAL PICTURE.**

Throughout this book, I make reference to the September 11th tragedy to highlight certain examples of the "doctrine of change" I could have used any of a number of other critical situations. **But September 11th represents one of the most critical situations that not only the United States had to experience but every nation on the face of this earth.**

Every action that we take, impacts on everyone and everything in our Universe and there is also an impact on our relationship with our spiritual self and with God.

The example of the pebble in the pond illustrates this point very vividly. If we can grasp this fundamental principle, we can then understand how, if we change our thoughts, we can change the world.

And so I invite each and every one who reads this book, to **STEP INTO THE FUTURE! The future is exciting and filled with glorious potential. Lets go!**

CHAPTER 5

The If It Ain't Broke Why Fix It Theory Of Change

Why the need for change?

Whenever I am required to give bad news to my patients, one question that I have to answer repeatedly is, "Why did this have to happen to me doctor?" Invariably my answer would be, "Because life was never meant to be always smooth and easy!"

It is because of winter that we are better able to appreciate spring. In the chapter, "The Power of Change" I related an anecdote about the old man and the sea to illustrate why some people change and others do not. It is a simple but true fact about life that it was meant to consist of peaks and valleys. Otherwise, we really have no purpose on this earth. God wouldn't need us.

How many of us dream of living the lives of movie stars or famous celebrities? I have pondered this question repeatedly. In trying to decipher the meaning of life, I have often wondered why God did not give us all equal amounts of material goods and the same physical attributes.

Why did God create so many diverse races? If God truly wanted there to be no change, why did He allow so many diverse races to exist? Why are some people so obscenely wealthy and others are forced to eke out a living? **The answer lies in the need for change.**

When God created Adam and Eve and placed them in the Garden of Eden, they were provided with every material thing that they needed. Boredom and the need for change led them to eat from the tree with the forbidden fruit. Adam and Eve wanted and needed change for their growth.

The problem is that the change they sought was not meaningful change for their personal growth and led to them being banished from the Garden of Eden. In fact the growth that they needed was not physical but spiritual growth. Physical growth would only have caused them to age and suffer all the diseases of aging. Spiritual growth on the other hand would have allowed them to continue to grow forever.

But consider what the consequence would have been if there was no apple for Adam and Eve to eat. Would you and I have been on this earth today? Would the world have grown to be what it is today? The quest for change and growth continues in our lives today. But like Adam and Eve, we have continued the same pattern of behavior as they

70

displayed, because of our lack of knowledge of the significance of meaningful change in our lives.

The reason Adam and Eve partook of the fruit of life was because of their need for change. They had frankly become bored with their meaningless existence and saw no opportunity for growth. *The reason for our very existence is the need for meaningful change.*

Why did God need Adam and Eve anyway? **Does God really need us with all of our negative and destructive behaviors?** But consider what if God had never created us? **Could God exist in a vacuum?** We need God just as much as God needs us. And who created the serpent to tempt Adam and Eve anyway? **The answer lies in the fact that the secret of life is all about the need for change, meaningful change.**

Did you ever wonder why Elvis Presley preferred to eat peanut butter sandwiches rather than filet mignon steaks; even though he could have afforded to eat the best steaks or lobster thermidor every day of his life? Have you ever wondered why so many celebrities who possess so much material wealth still appear to lead such miserable lives? Do you ever wonder how this could be?

The simple truth is that these people who have accomplished so much **fail** to see any need or opportunity to effect meaningful change in their lives. Consequently they become just as bored, just as depressed, just as frustrated and just as disenchanted with life as the poor hobo sleeping on the streets of Manhattan on a cold winter's night with nothing but some newspaper for cover and a cardboard box for a bed.

The ability to effect meaningful change is what permits us to continue to grow and instill purpose and meaning to our lives!

When I examine the lives of so many of the celebrities whose lives have followed the path of despair and destruction, I feel just as much sadness for them as I do for the single mother on the East side of Chicago who has to feed seven hungry children with a five hundred dollars a month social security check.

In each instance they lack the ability to effect meaningful change in their lives.

The celebrity who follows the path of self-destruction is just as unable to recognize, visualize or plan to effect meaningful change as the down and out destitute derelict in Manhattan or Somalia. In each instance they follow the path of decline and decay.

Do the names Robert Downey, Elvis, Whitney, Jimmie Hendrix and Karen Carpenter come to mind? I could name countless others among this group including Howard Hughes, Marilyn Munroe and numerous other celebrities whose lives spiraled downwards faster than a plane with suicidal terrorists on board.

These individuals like everyone else could have benefited from understanding and learning how to effect meaningful change in their lives.

What puzzles me is that these individuals with all their wealth have access to some of the best psychiatrists and psychologists in the world. So what's wrong with the picture?

Do you still question another book that seeks to teach others how to effect meaningful change? Can you see why I have chosen to write this book and why more books of this type are necessary?

Clearly no one was able to show these people how to effect meaningful change in their lives. Hopefully this book will serve such a needed purpose. **If there was no need for a book such as this, why do I have to teach my patients day in and day out how to effect meaningful change in their lives?**

Why do they return from the counselors requesting increasing doses in their anti-depressant medication or additions to the two dozens pills that they are already taking for treating their diabetes and heart disease and hypertension?

How many diet plans have the diet gurus not touted and how many diet pills have come on the market, only to be withdrawn because of the damage that has been done to those who have taken them? Something is very wrong with this picture!

In dealing with my own patients, I recognize that many of these individuals have suffered the same fate as many of the famous celebrities. **They have never been taught how to effect meaningful change, in their lives, in their relationships, in their businesses or organizations or in their spiritual being.**

This is indeed an unfortunate situation because as I have discovered, the concept of change is so simple to understand and the process of change is so simple to implement. It simply takes a **willingness** to learn the process.

We need to make paradigm shifts. What does this mean? This in fact is what change is all about. If we were to subscribe to the "don't fix it if it ain't broke" theory and most people do, we would hardly ever be inclined to make changes. We would never improve and we would never progress.

Would we really like to spend all of our lives on the beach catching fish all day long and basking in the sun? Be careful of what you wish for! **Too much sunshine causes skin cancer.**

The result of doing the same repetitive tasks all day, every day would be that we would continue with the same mundane and boring existence that most people face in their daily lives and the consequence of this is the unhappiness, hopelessness and depression that so many people in the world face today. This is the underlying cause of career burnout and employee dissatisfaction in companies.

I subscribe to the theory that LIFE IS ALL ABOUT CLIMBING MOUNTAINS. We need mountains in our lives to climb. There is nothing more exhilarating or spectacular than the view from the top of a mountain.

Picture yourself at the top of whatever little mountain you are most familiar with in your immediate vicinity and close your eyes and imagine the view around you. Then picture yourself on top of a mountain range in Arizona, the Rocky Mountains or the Andes and imagine the view below.

Continue to imagine yourself climbing higher and higher mountain peaks and imagining the spectacular views below. Try to picture the view if you will, from every mountaintop in the world. Sometimes it requires tremendous sacrifice and effort to climb a mountain but to the mountain climber, there is nothing more spectacular than the view from the top.

In our lifetime we can never exhaust ourselves of mountains to climb. This in essence is in some way what change is all about.

I try to tell my patients that life is all about peaks and valleys. **(The psychiatrists would prefer to call this bi-polar disorder and treat it with pills rather than showing people that life itself is all about peaks and valleys.)**

If the mountain climber when he/she reaches the top of the mountain decides to stay there, the view can become very boring. That is why mountain climbers are constantly seeking new peaks to challenge them.

I once lived in a country with some of the most beautiful beaches in the world, Barbados. People often ask me why I left Barbados to move to cold, snowy Michigan.

When I first moved to Barbados to live, I vowed that I would go to the beach every day. After the first year, I vowed that I would go to the beach every week. By the end of the second year, I swore that I would go to the beach every month. By the fourth year, I could not wait for family and friends to come visit me so that I could get an excuse to go to the beach.

After the fifth year or so, I would point my relatives and friends who were visiting, in the general direction of the beach! By the sixth year I let them find their own directions to the beach.

There are thousands of people who live in Barbados who do not even know how to swim! Similarly, I have encountered people who live in Michigan who have never left Michigan, far less travel to Ohio or Canada which are just across the border. Can you imagine how boring their lives must be? These are people who have never been willing or able to change.

I once paid for one such individual who had recently been diagnosed with cancer of the stomach, to go for a plane ride with her husband, who also had never been on a plane. Their excitement was something to behold when they returned. They were like kids who had been let loose in Toys 'R Us. They were so excited that they wanted to repeat the experience the next week.

I am also happy to say that that her cancer has been in remission for several years now and she is considered cured. **(I don't think that the plane ride had anything to do with her cancer being cured but it sure made her feel good!)**

I recently visited Sedona in Arizona one of the most mind altering places on earth. The majestic beauty of the mountains, the painted cliffs and the sheer awe-inspiring scenery overwhelmed me. I thought to myself, "This is surely what heaven must look like." When I mentioned to one of the owners of a souvenir shop how lucky she was to be able to live in such a spectacular place, she just shrugged and replied in the most nonchalant manner, "You don't have to live here all year long." The lack of change caused this individual to be unable to enjoy what for me was one of the grandest and most spectacular scenery on earth!

Just suppose that Henry Ford was content to continue riding in a Horse and Buggy all his life. Would we have had the motorcar today? I recently saw the future form of personal transportation in a recent television show. It is called the "Segway". Hopefully by the time this book is published, I will be able to afford living in the future with my new 'Segway.'

So what does this all mean? It means that change is a vital component of life. Change must occur for growth to take place. **Change is vitality**. The very process of life requires that meaningful change must be constantly occurring. When change no longer occurs in the human body, death sets in. **Change is also exciting!**

My advice to you if you belong to an organization, is that you had better demonstrate to others around you that you are still moving or someone is likely to call the undertakers to take you away.

How often have we not heard of people who were taken away by undertakers, and presumed to be dead when they were still in fact alive? The reason is that there was a perception that there was no activity occurring in those individuals; i.e. no apparent physiological change was taking place.

How does this relate to you, in your life; in your organization; in your community; in society; in your world; in your relation to God and your spiritual self?

Are you like those individuals who are effectively dead because they will not or cannot make the effort to change? Are your relationships like that? Are your communities, societies, and organizations like that? Is your world like that? Is your relationship with God like that?

Change is also about constantly striving to improve your spirituality? Are you still alive? Will you change (show some activity) so that others can recognize that you are still functioning?

The bubble mentality.

Living inside a bubble is a term that was introduced to me by one of my nieces. She accused her mother of living inside a bubble. Yet when I looked at my niece, if ever there was an individual who lived inside a bubble, she was the poster child for bubble dwellers.

She had so many fixed assumptions of her heritage and the society from which her mother had come that it was easier to demolish the Berlin Wall than to get her to abandon those fixed assumptions and to look at life with an open and uncluttered mind. **Before meaningful change can begin to happen, we all need to adopt an open mental model. We all need to get out of our bubbles.**

Bubbles can keep bad things out and away from the individuals within the bubble, as in the case of some children with immune deficiency diseases. But bubbles also keep out good things from entering and enriching the lives of the inhabitants of the bubble. And bubbles severely limit and restrict growth, physically, mentally and spiritually.

Economists and philosophers both speak of **OPEN** and **CLOSED systems**. A closed system is basically a dead system. No growth can occur in a **closed** system. An **open** system is one that will permit growth.

Picture a shark being raised in a small aquarium. My son once raised sharks in a small aquarium. The sharks could only grow as much as the size of the aquarium would permit them to grow. On the other hand if the sharks were allowed to grow in the ocean, those sharks would have had the opportunity to reach their maximal growth capacity.

As individuals, we can choose a mental model that is either **closed** or one that is **open**. If we choose the closed mental model, we limit our mental capacity to grow and soon we become devoid of new ideas (mental death). When this occurs, we become no different from those individuals who suffer from Alzheimer's disease. **Now that I think about it maybe this theory explains the cause of Alzheimer's disease?**

On the contrary, if we choose an open mental model, we allow ourselves the opportunity for maximal growth. And as many of us are aware, we only utilize a small fraction of our mental capacity during our lifetime.

The opportunity for mental growth is therefore virtually limitless. **The capacity for growth is only limited by how great we can dream.** We simply need to allow ourselves to live within an open mental model.

Our capacity to operate within an open mental model is limited by the fixed assumptions that so many of us hold. Unlike the little train that said **"I think I can I think I can"**, many of us operate with the **"I think I can't, I think I can't!"** philosophy. Learning how to effect meaningful change teaches us how to think, **"I can"**.

I believe that we all need to learn how to effect meaningful change in our individual lives, our personal relationships, our organizations, our societies and in our spiritual being. Not only are we capable of learning how to make these changes within us but also we are capable of learning how to and **we do need to, teach others** how to make similar changes. **It would be pointless if only we changed and no one else did.**

Invest in change. Change yourself and learn how to help others do the same! The power that will come your way will be like no other power on earth and the return on your investment will exceed anything that the stock market ever yielded even during its boom period.

CHAPTER 6

Power Of Change

The power to change lies within each and every one of us. Each individual has the capacity to change and every individual has the ability to change others. We have the power and we simply need to harness that power and use it creatively. But beyond that, we do not only possess the power to effect meaningful change in us and others, **we have the moral obligation to do so.**

Using the analogy of the ripples created by a pebble in a pond, if we can change ourselves, we will automatically change others. Can you therefore imagine how much power we each and every one of us possess? One small action that is taken in Lubbock, Texas, can influence major changes in Tajikistan or Azerbaijan. *Prior to September 11th, many of us couldn't pronounce these words, much less to be able to spell them*

The Doctrine of Change teaches that each of us has the capacity to change ourselves. Each of us also has the capacity to influence change in others. Each of us has power that we can share with others to facilitate change.

Like the flowing waters of the powerful Niagara Falls that generates electricity for large parts of Canada and the USA, we all possess the power to change us and others. But whether we harness that power and use it for good is dependent on our willingness to learn how to do so and our capacity to put that power to good use.

I grew up in Guyana, a land of incredible beauty and where one of the biggest waterfalls in the world, the Kaiteur Falls, is located,. For years the various governments of Guyana have spoken of using the power of the mighty Kaiteur Falls to generate power for Guyana. It has been over thirty years that this discussion has been ongoing in Guyana. **The people of Guyana still continue to experience rolling blackouts on a daily basis. Why is this so?**

In spite of all the brilliant minds that have emerged from Guyana, the biggest obstacle lies in the lack of the will to effect meaningful change that causes the people of Guyana to continue to suffer the hardships of daily rolling blackouts. The government and people of Guyana clearly see the potential benefits of the power of the rolling waters of the mighty Kaiteur Falls and the government of Canada offered many years ago to help them harness the power of the Kaiteur Falls. Both parties could have benefited significantly from the collaborative effort.

I am positive that the majority of people in Guyana do not enjoy the discomfort and hardships of daily rolling blackouts. Clearly they can also see the need for change. So why then do they still continue to live in the same way as the pioneers who first came to settle in the USA?

Obviously in addition to the unwillingness to change on the part of some, there has also never been a good plan. Consequently, without a plan there is also no hope of implementing the plan.

So too, in our quest to change us and others, we need to follow the six steps outlined in this book before we can even hope to implement meaningful change.

When meaningful change occurs, there are only winners; there are no losers.

For meaningful change to occur, we must first recognize the need to change, visualize the benefits to the change we desire and the consequences if we make no change, accept the need to change, desire or be willing to change, plan or develop a mental map of how to change and finally implement the plan.

There must also be a willingness on the part of all concerned to effect meaningful change. **Change that is forced upon others can never be meaningful or long lasting!** This is probably a significant reason why there has been no peace in the Middle East for centuries. **Each side in the dispute has sought to impose its will on the other side**. The result is the lifelong conflict that is seen in that part of the world.

For years, in Ireland the conflict between Catholics and Protestants continued because each side sought to kill the other into submission to the other's will. Finally they realized that they were only succeeding in destroying each other.

At the time of writing this book, there is a ceasefire between the two factions in Northern Ireland. Hopefully that is as a result of the desire on the part of each side to seek meaningful solutions to their problems. Otherwise we can anticipate with more than a reasonable degree of certainty that the ceasefire will only be temporary.

This is also why our criminal justice system has failed us. Our jails are more crowded than ever. Our justice system seeks to force the criminals to change and no adequate system is in place to teach the criminals why and how to effect meaningful change in their lives. We speak of rehabilitation as if putting people in jail will have a magical effect in changing them.

Rehabilitation requires the knowledge of how to effect meaningful change in others. How many of our rehabilitators can claim to understand the principles of change as I have outlined in this book. If they do, then they have not been utilizing the principles.

Why else are our jails more crowded than ever and many criminals are kept at home with tethers? Judges issue lenient sentences on serious criminals not

because they do not think that the punishment should be more severe but because the prison system is too overcrowded. We spend millions, if not billions of dollars building new jails and supporting criminals in the jails.

There are those who would like us to believe that the use of tethers is meaningful change. Absolute rubbish! This is purely a matter of convenience.

Soon we may be asked to share our homes with the criminals and we will be told about the wonderful changes that have been made in the criminal justice system.

Is it our problem whether meaningful change occurs in our justice system? You bet your life it is! And I mean that in more than a figurative sense. I mean that both literally and figuratively. When criminals are allowed to live among us in society, without being taught why and how to effect meaningful change, our very lives and livelihood are put at risk. I have asked the question before and ask it again, "Can the blind lead the blind?"

If the guardians of our destiny do not understand how to effect meaningful change in themselves, how can they teach others how to do the same? "Can the blind lead the blind?" I ask yet again. The harsh truth is that in so many aspects of our lives, where meaningful change is needed, we have the blind leading the blind. And in many instances, we have the <u>dead</u> leading the blind.

In my practice, I take care of youth who belong to a program called 'Boysville of Michigan.' The inmates of 'Boysville are youth, boys and girls who have been sent to this program because of various misdemeanors and criminal activities that they have indulged in.

I agreed to accept these youth into my practice because no other physician in my town would accept them. I have found these kids to be the most well-mannered and polite youngsters that I have ever dealt with.

They are always neatly dressed and clean. Whenever they come to me, they wear uniforms of either blue or white shirts and khaki or blue 'Dickies' pants. **Many of these kids have committed to going to college. Many have actually gone on to college**.

Remember that these kids were the same ones who were failing in their schools and in society. It is a pleasure for me to take care of these kids. The caregivers at this institution clearly understand what meaningful change is all about.

So why is it that our traditional school system is failing? Why are the teachers in our traditional schools so stressed out that many of them are seeking alternative professions. The answer lies in the inability of the system and the teachers to understand the concept of how and why meaningful change is necessary. Yet it is within the same system that 'Boysville of Michigan' continues to flourish.

There is a clear lesson to be learnt here. When I see the success of a program such as 'Boysville of Michigan' and I see the failures in our traditional school system, I begin to wonder whether we have our priorities and our values reversed.

The prevalence of preventable diseases continues to rise every year. The result is a tremendous cconomic burden on our society. Keeping criminals locked up in jails and building more jails without teaching the criminals how to effect meaningful change imposes a tremendous financial burden on our society.

We are wasting scarce economic resources. We all pay for this tremendous wastage in the form of higher income taxes and pot-holes filled roads and increased insurance premiums and so on and so on.

Can you see now why it is our problem? Can you understand why we need to learn how to effect meaningful change in us and learn how to teach others how to do the same? *The economic consequences of not understanding how to effect meaningful change is costing our society billions of dollars.*

We can save ourselves a lot of heartache, a lot of stress and we can save our communities those **billions** of wasted dollars. And we will be immensely richer because every dollar saved comes right back into our pockets in the form of reduced taxes, reduced insurance premiums and improvements in our security and our society. **The amazing fact is that it would not cost society one cent more to do the right thing. We are often told how much money it would cost to fix the various broken systems, healthcare, justice, education etc. What a load of baloney. Any economist worth his salt could show that through using the principles outlined in this book, the cost would be minimal and the gains would be stupendous. And we will all be winners, ten times over.**

There are no losers when meaningful change occurs.

For us to become effective change agents, we need to become futurists. We must develop the capacity to look into the future and predict the need for change **before** that need arises.

We need to improve our negotiating skills. We cannot influence change in others if we lack proper negotiating skills. After all, very few people will change willingly. As I have stated previously, change involves a certain element of risk and uncertainty. We will only be able to convince others to change if we can show them that change will allow them to accomplish their perceived goals.

We do not need to be trained economists to see the tremendous economic benefits of meaningful change. But if we could understand certain basic economic principles it would help us to develop a stronger conviction as to why we need to teach others why and how to change and why resistance to implementing meaningful change is costing us.

If we understand basic economic concepts we would realize that the unwillingness to change could hurt us physically and financially. **Ask anyone who has gone through a divorce whether this is true or not! Yet some of the most successful businessmen have failed to apply the principles of change in their personal lives. Just take a look around you to see what I mean.**

This lack of understanding of **basic economic principles** is a major stumbling block in the medical profession today. The reason that physicians as a group remain most resistant to change is that many of them (us) do not have a clear grasp of fundamental economic principles. I am not referring to the knowledge of how to make money. *Any fool can strike it rich overnight from purchasing a winning lottery ticket or hitting the jackpot in a casino.*

It requires a certain degree of knowledge of basic economic principles to understand how to utilize our resources maximally and efficiently and to get maximal benefits from the money we already possess.

If more physicians understood this, they would recognize that if we do not change our approach to medical care, that we will continue to frustrate ourselves and some of us will be putting ourselves out of business.

The fact of the matter is that many physicians have already put themselves out of business voluntarily, through early retirement. These physicians could not see themselves changing, or failed to see the possibility of them being able to make meaningful change in the system or for the system to be changed for the better. **Since become a futurist, I have removed the word retirement from my vocabulary except when writing books. The word retirement to me is now like a four letter word**.

As far as the medical establishment is concerned, those physicians who refuse to embrace change are effectively dead. **Fortunately many of them were able to recognize their death and withdrew from the system voluntarily**.

Unfortunately, there are many still within the system, many of whom are near death but still remain in the system and are creating a tremendous stench. These physicians continue to practice medicine the same way that it was practiced fifty years ago. **They are proud to announce how well they are doing financially and resent any suggestion of change.**

My God! **Can you imagine how dead these individuals are?** And they have been dead for many years! They are walking zombies. **Could it be that the movie, 'Dead Man Walking" was based on the lives of some of these people?**

Sure they utilize new technologies and newer medicines but the fact remains that their methods remain the same as they were fifty years ago. I recently heard an esteemed physician state with great regret in his voice that **"medicine is not what it used to** be". Many would like for us to return to the "good old days".

The world has changed but we would like to return to the "good old days". The world has changed but we are still employing nineteenth century techniques. **The reason dinosaurs became extinct is that they failed to adapt to the new age.** *If we are to survive in whatever we do, we must adapt to our new environment, whatever the environment.* But as stated earlier, we can **choose** the environment that we would like to be in or **we can be placed** in an environment that we resent, **like animals in a zoo.**

We must change if we are not to follow the course of the dinosaurs and the simple truth is that the power to change lies within each and every one of us. We have to learn how to harness that power and use it effectively, just like the power of the mighty Niagara Falls has been harnessed to generate electricity for half of Canada and parts of New York.

On the other hand, we could fail to harness and release that power within us, just as in the case of the Kaiteur Falls in Guyana and we will continue to experience the rolling blackouts in our lives.

The ability to change us and to influence change in others requires learning and applying certain basic skills. These skills are the **tools** that we use to conceive change and then plan and implement change. **It requires that we become futurists, skilled negotiators, economists and good marketers.**

As difficult as this might seem, it really is quite simple. But like change itself, it requires a willingness to learn these techniques and patience and perseverance and constant practice.

The purpose of this book is to help those who are willing to learn, how to do so. And as I have said repeatedly, we **all** have the capacity to change and each one of us has the capacity to change many others. We simply need the willingness to embrace change.

> **We need to learn how to harness the power within each of us and to change and show others how to harness the power within them.**

CHAPTER 7

The Power To Influence Change

It is human nature to resist change. Whenever people are faced with the decision to change, their reluctance to do so usually results from their perception that there is some risk involved in change or they are unwilling to sacrifice what they already possess for some uncertain result. Change to many people usually implies risk taking or a threat to their security.

Some groups and some individuals are generally more resistant to change than others. **Physicians as individuals and as a group have the reputation of being most resistant to change. This group cherishes its autonomy and any attempts to influence change in them is invariably perceived as a threat to their autonomy.**

And yet, because of the rapid advances in medical technology, physicians should be the group most willing to embrace change. I mentioned in an earlier section of this book the statement made by the keynote speaker at the commencement address of a graduating class of medical students. The speaker said, **"Fifty percent of the things that you were taught in medical school would eventually be proved to be wrong. The problem is that we do not know which fifty percent it is."**

Another speaker when addressing another group of medical students, remarked **that in ten years time, fifty percent of what they learnt in medical school would be obsolete. The most recent comment that I have heard on this subject is that, "by the end of their residency periods, medical students would find that fifty percent of what they learned in medical school would be obsolete.**

If this trend continues, we could soon expect to hear that by the time the professors have finished their lectures that fifty percent of what they just heard in the classroom would be obsolete.

If we assume that as physicians fifty percent of our learning would be obsolete in five years and additionally that no one knows which fifty percent of our learning is false, why then is it that we as physicians, as an esteemed group are so resistant to change?

Consider the hypothetical case of Physician X and Mr. Jones a patient. Physician X is asked to see Mr. Jones in the hospital after Mr. Jones is admitted with a severe case of pancreatitis.

Upon discharge, Mr. Jones wants to go to an extended care facility where he feels that he would not impose a burden on his wife since he feels that he needs some additional care. The physician on the other hand feels that Mr. Jones could be well taken care at home by visiting nurses and that this would be less costly to the insurance company; thereby reducing the physician's and the insurance company's total cost for providing care to Mr. Jones.

Since Mr. Jones belongs to a Managed Care Organization, the doctor feels that he is practicing cost effective medicine without compromising the quality of care. Furthermore the physician is particularly annoyed that Mr. Jones has opted to go to utilize a facility where the physician's primary practice is not based and under the managed care contract this is costing the physician more for providing care to the patient.

He insists that Mr. Jones should in future only go to the hospital where his managed care group is contracted.

Mr. Jones on the other hand feels that since his insurance company is paying his bills and there is no apparent additional cost to him directly that he could go to whichever hospital he chooses. Also being unwell and being at home he feels would be an unnecessary burden on his elderly wife even though home help care is being offered. Additionally he prefers to be in an extended care facility.

Clearly both parties have a legitimate reason for their preference of care and with a little bit of reasoning and a willingness to be open to a change of views they could well resolve their problems and both parties could have a bit of what they each want.

Instead neither party would bend to the other's point of view and consequently they become involved in a classic shouting match. Name-calling occurs and the physician decides that he is going to terminate his care of the patient. Mr. Jones in turn decides that he was going to leave the practice anyway.

In addition Mr. Jones decides that he will report the physician to the medical board for abusive behavior. He demands an apology from the physician who is adamant that he will not be doing so.

A third party is asked to intervene in the situation. It is clear that the hospital has already more or less determined the way they prefer to resolve the problem. **There is the underlying not so very subtle hint that the best solution (for the hospital) would be to have the physician apologize to Mr. Jones**. This would be the simplest solution but definitely not one that would result in any type of meaningful change by either party.

The effect of such a feeble solution would be to **force** upon the physician the need to change his behavior. I have clearly stated **that force does not result in meaningful**

change. Physician X may change his behavior for a short period of time and he would clearly resent whoever makes him do so.

The chances of him repeating his behavior in a similar situation in future remains extremely high. **Because of the managed care environment in which we operate today, such a possibility of the same type of situation repeating itself occurs on an almost daily basis to all of us**.

The chance of Mr. Jones continuing to demonstrate a laissez-faire attitude to health care costs also remains high. No one even suggests that Mr. Jones need to reconsider his attitude to the need for a change of his behavior.

Physician X in his way is also trying to force Mr. Jones to change. Mr. Jones fails to see the need to change, sees no benefits to change and uses some fairly colorful language to indicate that he has no intention to change. The end result is the confrontational situation that ensues.

What is needed here is a change of the mental model of both parties so that meaningful change could be reached by and on behalf of all concerned, Mr. Jones, Physician X, the hospital and the HMO.

For meaningful change to occur, all parties need to recognize the need for change, to accept the need for change, to be willing to change, to see the benefits of change, to plan for change and then to implement change.

Eventually an arbitrator has to be called in to convince both parties that what is needed is just a slight change in attitude towards each other and they would both emerge as winners. **If this scenario seems familiar to you, it is because it is occurring everywhere managed care is present. Right now as you read this book, an identical situation is occurring in your own institution. It probably happened to you yesterday. Did it?**

Brokering Change

Consider another situation that actually occurred to me. During one of my hospital rounds, I happened to make an innocent comment to one of the nurses in one unit of our hospital. I mentioned that she looked very relaxed in what she was doing. It was an entirely benign comment, meant more to be an icebreaker than anything else and to initiate some friendly conversation. Her response astonished me and provided another lesson about the process and the power of change.

She told me that she was far from relaxed and that she was very stressed out. In keeping with my philosophy of change, I told her that maybe she needed a change from her job. I suggested to her that she might want to consider doing something different for a short while until she felt better.

She mentioned that she was seriously considering such a move and then proceeded to tell me that several of the more senior nurses had already left the department. This statement was a total surprise to me. I had not realized that such a critical situation existed in the department.

I became genuinely concerned at that point and felt that this was not a situation that was in the best interest of the nurses, the physicians, the hospital, or the patients. I knew for example that the quality of care for my own patients was going to suffer if the experienced nurses became replaced by less experienced nurses.

Not only were my nights on call going to be more interrupted but also with decreased quality of care, more medical errors were likely. This would mean at the very least, increased lengths of hospital stays resulting in increased cost of medical care. In the managed care setting this could be disastrous.

At worst, there would likely be increased liabilities for the hospital and me if medical errors were committed. The consequences of this would likely be increased premiums, which would mean me having to work harder...and so on and so forth.

An innocent and very simple remark revealed what was potentially a major problem with far reaching implications. I decided to pursue the matter a little further and asked the nurse to clarify some of the problems that were leading to such intense dissatisfaction in her colleagues that would make a talented and skilled group of individuals want to give up the careers that they had spent so many years developing.

By this time, several other nurses had joined the discussion and **I was afraid that I was about to instigate a revolution and I was in grave danger of being perceived as the enemy and faced the prospect that I might be assassinated**. Nevertheless, I was determined to pursue the matter.

They explained to me that there were several problems in the department and they felt that no one cared to address their problems. *They were also afraid that if they attempted to address the issues that they would be victimized.* One of the problems they stated was that there were many more residents (new medical graduates) on the unit and the nurses felt that these residents were not well supervised. The nurses felt that this was jeopardizing patient care.

In addition, after the World Trade center attack of September 11th, two of these residents were allegedly observed to be cheering. This further infuriated the nurses and they felt that someone should address the issue. They also proceeded to inform me of some of the other problems related to equipment etc. They felt that their problems and concerns were not being addressed and they were becoming increasingly frustrated.

Their perception of their inability to effect change is what was causing increased

stress and frustration, resulting in what could develop into a potentially critical situation.

At this point, one of the nurses asked me what department I was in charge of since I had offered to help them deal with their problem. *I informed them that I really was not in charge of anything but I understood the problems and I was willing to help them broker the change they wanted.*

I offered to show them how they could achieve the changes that they desired without jeopardizing their careers **and help the hospital in the process**. In other words, I offered to show them how to effect **meaningful** change.

The solution to what at first appeared to be a problem of potentially major proportions was to convince all parties concerned that changes were needed and that these changes were eminently achievable and that the effect of the changes would not only be in everyone's best interest but I could show through the concept of inter-connectedness that everyone would be a winner.

The first thing that I had to do was to assure them that the fixed assumptions that they would be victimized were not valid and needed to be discarded. This was by no means an easy task but I did finally convince one of these nurses that they could make some real and beneficial changes. After she had been convinced, others followed.

I showed them how important their role was in the organization. I showed them how they were connected through their work with every other department of the hospital. I showed them how every one loses when the quality of care deteriorates. I showed them how the administration and they both stood to benefit from correcting the underlying problems.

I showed them why the administration should care whether the nurses were happy in their work. And I offered to help them approach the administration to help them deal with their problems.

When the nurses recognized the potential that they had for effecting meaningful change and that someone genuinely cared about their problems, the resultant effect was a more satisfied group of nurses with improved morale. This definitely resulted in better patient care. Improved quality care resulted in better outcomes and improved cost-savings to the hospital, physicians, patients and insurance companies. Every one was a winner!

The new residents were afforded better supervision. I suggested that some one should point out to the two residents who were allegedly seen cheering the World Trade Center bombing that the resulting effect on the national economy would likely be a cut in health care funding since money would have to be diverted to improvements in national security and this would likely come from the health care budget.

This could result in fewer slots for medical residents and furthermore when these residents were finished with their training the chances of them finding the jobs that they wanted would be decreased.

The result of a simple intervention averted a major crisis, resulted in improved quality care and resulted in major cost-savings. Everyone was a winner, including hopefully those two cheering residents. Hopefully they would have learnt to reshape their mental model and realize that the actions of the terrorists on September 11th did not exempt them from the effects of the tragedy of September 11th.

Hopefully by understanding the principle of inter-connectedness, their view of their relation with the rest of the world will be changed and they in turn will be able to influence change in others around the world.

Who would ever have thought that a simple question such as asking a nurse how she was feeling would have the capacity to influence such wide-ranging change?

And who would think that someone without any titles has the capacity to make such a major difference? The lesson to be learnt here is that anyone who takes the time to invest in learning how to effect meaningful change has as much power as the heads of companies or organizations.

The chapter, 'Leaders and Change', shows that leaders in organizations do not need titles. We simply need to step forward when we see something that needs to be fixed or something that would be helpful to the group and as the Nike ad says, 'Just do it!' With a simple slogan like that, is it any wonder that Nike is the leader in its field?

CHAPTER 8

Negotiating Change

The Walk in the Woods Theory

Every now and then, **more now than then**, you will encounter someone or some situation that needs to be changed. You may see the need for another person to change but the other party absolutely refuses to change.

As a practicing physician, I have spent the past 28 years trying to influence meaningful change in my patients. In the medical profession, that is our job every day of our working lives. The harsh truth is that we as a group have failed horribly to teach our patients how to effect meaningful change simply because so many of us have never understood the philosophy of change.

If we are to be more effective in helping others to effect meaningful change, we need to first acquire the tools to help us in our task. We also need to learn and understand the philosophy of change and the process of change and constantly practice using the tools at our disposal.

The question is, **"how do you deal with those individuals who absolutely refuse to change"**? The situation that physicians face is no different from the heads of organizations or institutions or companies trying to influence others to change. It is no different from a situation where one party in a failing relationship seeks to get the other party to change and the other party bluntly refuses to do so.

It is no different when you love another and the feeling is not reciprocated. Unrequited love exists when you love someone and he/she would not give you the time of day and you desperately desire to show her that you are the right person for him/her.

As physicians, our entire lives are spent trying to influence others to make meaningful change in their health only to be met with forceful resistance. We try to influence change in our patients. We try to influence change in our hospitals. We try to influence change in HMOs and other third party payers. We try to influence change in our government. Have we succeeded? I don't think so if we consider the current state of medical care, being what it is today. **If anyone believes otherwise, I can still find more beachfront property in Arizona for sale.**

We physicians should truly be the experts in teaching others how to effect meaningful change. But are we? **GM and Chrysler, IBM and Microsoft should be consulting** us for advice on how to motivate their employees. Do they? If not, why not?

Prior to studying the philosophy of change, I had my own techniques for dealing with these situations of resistance. Like so many of my colleagues, whenever I could not get patients to follow my <u>orders</u>, I simply labeled them 'non-compliant' and gave them notice to seek help elsewhere.

Isn't it a strange coincidence that in hospitals when physicians write instructions for the patients that it is done on a physician "order" form. We do not make recommendations, we give "orders." And we are disappointed when our patients will not follow our "orders." Where else but in the military and in prison do people willingly follow orders?

Since learning the process of change, my approach is different and the word 'non-compliant' no longer exists in my vocabulary. I have also eliminated the word 'retirement' from my vocabulary. I am all the better for it and I am writing this book to teach others how to do the same. For me to label someone as non-compliant is to admit failure by me. *And I would be debunking my belief that everyone needs to and can be shown why and how to effect meaningful change.*

Whenever we come upon someone or some circumstance that needs change, we can approach the problem from one of two aspects. **We can force or try to force the other parties to change**.

As I have stated repeatedly, **this does not result in meaningful change**. Unfortunately, this is the approach that most physicians adopt when dealing with patients. We give the patients orders and tell them, *"It is either our way or the highway."* When these individuals do not follow our instructions to a T, they are then labeled as 'noncompliant.'

The alternative and better approach is to **teach** the other party why change is beneficial and how to effect such change. **This requires time, patience and perseverance. Most physicians will say, with a large degree of truth, that they simply do not have the time to spend with these patients. After all, our reimbursements are such that we have to increase our numbers or so we think.**

I suggest that if we invest our time wisely and teach these patients properly how to effect meaningful change, then the returns, economically, financially, emotionally and spiritually, will be far greater than the increased revenue generated purely from handing out pills or performing expensive and often unnecessary tests on these patients. As I show in this book, meaningful change results in tremendous economic gains through more efficient practices. We should not fear change.

In order to develop our effectiveness in helping us and others to make meaningful change, we need to acquire certain tools. We need to learn and develop basic negotiation skills and some marketing skills. After all, getting people who are unwilling to change requires some negotiation and eventually, we must obtain their 'buy-in.' We are after all dealing with the **business** of life since **change is the basis of life**. I have discovered that anyone can learn these basic skills and it is not necessary to be a business major to learn these simple techniques.

If simply being proficient in negotiation and marketing and economics was all it took to be able to influence meaningful change, then there would be no divorces among this group of people. There would be fewer divorces and broken relationships among economists and negotiators and marketing people. Right? Of course not! We all know that this is not so. However, the more proficient we become in utilizing these techniques, we are then provided with the tools that will help us to be able to successfully effect meaningful change.

But above all, in addition to acquiring basic negotiation, marketing and economic skills, it is absolutely necessary to understand the philosophy of change and learn and understand the process of change and apply it as I have demonstrated in the chapter, **"The Magical Mirror Experiment."**

The technique of teaching others how to make meaningful change is extremely simple and I will not complicate the process by making the discussion difficult. I will try to keep the technique of teaching how to effect meaningful change as simple as possible since my objective is to help as many people as possible to become competent at not only changing themselves but also in learning how to bring about meaningful change in others.

I acquired some of the tools from the best of the best and I whole-heartedly recommend them to anyone who seeks to develop competence in learning and becoming skilled in the art of negotiation and marketing.

I acquired the tools that I needed to teach others how to effect meaningful change from **Leonard Marcus PhD of Harvard University and Eric Berkowitz of the University of Massachusetts. I acquired the tools from these outstanding teachers during my participation in programs organized by the American College of Physician Executives.**

I was exposed to Hugh Long PhD of Tulane University, whose knowledge of the economics of medicine exceeds that of anyone else with whom I have come in contact. Of course, as I have stated earlier, Leland Kaiser PhD converted me to futurism. Roger Schenke M.D. gave me the tools to help me use my skills within an organizational and institutional setting.

All of these esteemed scholars are widely published and anyone wishing to go into more depth in learning how to use these tools should seek out books by these gentlemen. But the purpose of this book is not to develop your economic or negotiation or marketing skills. The purpose of this book is to teach you how to develop your skills in helping to bring about meaningful change.

I took the tools that these gentlemen provided me with and honed and sharpened them, developed my own philosophy of change and combined these skills and adapted them for my own purposes. The result is a tremendously different approach by me, to medical care and to my patients and to life in general. This book was produced to help others achieve their maximum potential and is the consequence of my changed approach and the results of my study and understanding of the philosophy of meaningful change.

Making changes in oneself is a most difficult task in itself. Getting others to change can be a Herculean task at best. *Sometimes in trying to teach the process of change to others, I felt that Hercules had an easier job cleaning out the Aegean stables than what I was trying to do.*

But with each success that I have seen from implementing my techniques, I feel that I obtain more satisfaction from what I do than Hercules did cleaning up horse manure.

I remember how difficult it was trying to get my children to do some of the things that I wanted them to do when they were growing up. If only I had understood the process of change and learnt the tools of negotiation, I could have saved myself many years of frustration. I also would have done a much better job of raising my children.

I could have also avoided all the Tums and ulcer medications of which I participated freely during their formative years.

I cannot tell you how I regret the many games of golf I missed because I did not learn the art of negotiation in the early years of my marriage. I could never convince my wife that the grass did not absolutely need to be cut on the same day that the guys were going out playing golf. Had I learnt the art of negotiation and had I been able to get in all those games of golf that I missed, I could have posed a major challenge to Tiger Woods today (with my arthritis and all.) Tiger doesn't know how lucky he is not having to contend with me as a golfer!

Anyone who has ever attempted to get others to change certain behaviors will understand how difficult it is to achieve this especially when the other party is resistant to change. Change naturally carries with it the element of uncertainty and this means risk. Change also implies the opportunity for loss of something that others cherish.

Change of the status quo removes a certain element of security. So how do we convince others that change is necessary and that change is ultimately beneficial?

Conviction in what you are doing plus constant practice is necessary to master the art of negotiation and the art of selling and marketing. Eventually, teaching

others the benefits of change becomes like second nature to you.

The greater the required change, the greater is the resistance to change. This means that we must be better skilled in the art of negotiation and marketing. How many physicians will honestly claim that they possess these skills naturally? These are for the most part, learned skills

Do not be afraid of learning how to acquire and master the use of these tools. I am not ashamed to say that I learned from the best and I will show by use of examples how simple it is to acquire and master these skills!

Since change carries with it risk of loss, negotiation skills requires a visionary approach. We need to be able to visualize what we are trying to show the individual requiring change and to show her/him the benefits of change.

We need to show the individual(s) or group that we are attempting to change that there will be **NO LOSS**. If the individual or group perceives **any** possibility of loss, resistance to change increases. We also need to show them the **gain** that results from meaningful change. Why should anyone who professes to enjoy smoking wish to change her habit, simply because **'the doctor said so.'**

I am aware that many people hold members of the medical profession in reverence and look upon us in a God-like manner. **But even God couldn't get Adam and Eve to be compliant. Or could he, but simply left the choices up to us? People must be shown why they would benefit from and be taught how to make meaningful change before they will be willing to do so.**

There is no pill that would assist with meaningful LONG-TERM change in people's negative behaviors. *Any pill that claims to do this does so by what constitutes chemical restraint and is really a violation of the civil liberties of individuals.* **I am surprised that the ACLU hasn't got involved in this issue yet in our schools. Instead they are more concerned about keeping out meaningful and positive attitudes out of our schools in the name of separation of church and state. Yet when we face a calamity such as September 11th, everyone starts praying and asking, "God save us all." How stupid or how blind do we think God is?**

We must constantly hold in the forefront that change is perceived to carry risk and the perception for potential loss. In my own study and understanding of the process of change it became patently clear that **change is vital for growth and gain**, but many individuals and organizations are reluctant to accept change because of their conservative nature.

So how **do** we convince others to change? I first learnt of the 'walk in the woods' from **Leonard Marcus PhD**. The principle of the 'walk in the woods' is to get people to identify a problem and to look beyond **selfish interests** (as opposed to **self-interest**) to seek a workable solution to the problem. The objective is to take them through a series of steps to get them to the point of considering **aligned interest** before seeking solutions to their problems.

To get to the point of considering aligned interest and finding solutions to their problem the individuals take 'a walk in the woods,' where in the peace and tranquility each party is allowed to get to know each other better in a more relaxed setting. Through familiarization with each other, each party then identifies common bonds that link them together and they become more willing to seek compromise.

In trying to show others why meaningful change makes sense and is rewarding, we help them by taking them through the same path as the 'walk in the woods.' I ask the people in whom I am trying to influence meaningful change, to examine their current state of affairs and to first identify whatever is the problem that needs to be addressed.

For example, when dealing with individuals who are having problems with their relationships, I encourage each party to put aside their selfish interests and consider how meaningful change would help them both to achieve what they really are seeking, which usually is the preservation of the relationship.

As I have stated repeatedly the principles and process of change are identical in every aspect of life. In this present discussion, we could elect to substitute a business or an organization for a personal relationship and the discussion remains the same.

The parties then move on from looking at things from the perspective of their **selfish interest** to looking at the interest of each other or their **self-interest and how the action of each party could adversely affect the other**. They are shown why finding a solution to their perceived problem would allow each other to co-exist. The next step in the walk is to show each party how collaboration or lack of it could adversely affect the group as a whole. This is the **enlarged interest**.

They are also shown how collaboration would benefit them as well as the organization. At the next stop in the 'walk in the woods' the parties attempt to find items of **enlightened interest** that would point them in the direction that they seek to be going.

From this point they are then **able to find common ground or aligned interest** before seeking a solution to their problems. **The solution usually falls into place easily thereafter.**

When each party sees the potential for gain and that no one is benefiting at the expense of the other the potential for meaningful change becomes a reality.

I have to confess that there have been occasions where, when dealing with some individuals, rather than taking those individuals for a walk in the woods, I felt like taking them behind the woodshed and dealing with them there; as in the case of a young miscreant who insisted that he wanted to be just like his father who was a drug addict and in jail. He said this to me in no uncertain terms.

This young man at age sixteen weighed over three hundred pounds and had already run afoul of the law on several occasions. The only redeeming factor was that he was in the care of some excellent people at one of the better rehabilitative programs and from their results, I knew that they understood how to effect meaningful change. So I knew that there was hope for him.

To simplify the above discussion about the 'walk in the woods' it would be easier to look at some actual case studies to see how problems were addressed and dealt with.

Annie get your gun.

As a practicing physician I will use an example of a situation which we as physicians encounter every day.

One of my patients whom we shall call Annie, had a habit of showing up in the Emergency Department of our local hospital on an almost daily basis, for some of the most trivial problems.

This is a problem that is also common with the nurses in the hospital. These nurses would show up in the Emergency Department after their work shift, for treatment of sore throats and runny noses and other minor problems. Getting these individuals to change their behaviors was an even greater task than getting Americans to stop super sizing their fries while simultaneously trying to lose weight. Breaking down the Berlin wall was a piece of cake compared to getting these individuals to reverse their negative behaviors.

Their argument against going to their primary care physician's office was that it was more convenient to go to the ER. Furthermore, according to their logic, who stood to lose anyway? After all, they had paid their premiums and the Insurance Company was the one who would have to pay for the ER visits anyway. And what was the difference whether the money was paid to the ER rather than the doctor's office. '**You doctors only want us to come to your offices so that you can make more money. You are just a bunch of greedy *#*!**%# any way.**

In other words, these individuals acting out of **"selfish interests"** perceived that the doctors were the ones acting out of their own selfish interests. In truth, physicians also when they seek to correct the problem, also only see the problem and the solution from their own selfish perspective. **This is why the problem is usually never adequately addressed and each party blames the other and both parties curse managed care.**

The problem in this particular case was in knowing how to first take these individuals beyond the point of **"selfish interest"** to one of **"self-interest"** with the ultimate goal being to take each party to a position of identifying **aligned interests** thereby leading to an agreement that would be mutually satisfying for solving the problem.

Using the principle of 'the walk in the woods' each party has an opportunity to stop at various points in the walk and smell the roses and listen to the crickets chirping, look at deer and rabbits and basically get to know each other a little better.

In moving from <u>selfish interest</u> to <u>self-interest</u>, each party examines how the problem is adversely affecting each other. They next move on to another area where they look at things from a broader perspective, that is, they examine <u>enlarged interests</u>. Here they move from examining how the problem is affecting each party to seeing how others are affected and how it is hindering progress of the group as a whole. From here they move to another area where they both start looking for aspects where each party can do things differently to take them closer to finding a solution to the problem. Here they begin considering <u>enlightened interests</u>.

The next stop in the walk is where they see benefits to everyone by adopting a unified position. This is where they identify <u>aligned interests</u>. Once they have reached this point in their walk, they are able to come up with a <u>solution</u> that is agreeable to all parties. This is where the walk in the woods ends.

I pointed out to Annie that because of escalating costs in the Medicaid program and with her being enrolled with Medicaid, that she was in danger of losing her Medicaid benefits, since the State of Michigan was cutting back on benefits for Medicaid recipients.

I showed her how it would be in **her** best interest if she took an active role in contributing to keeping down the cost of medical care. I showed her the **economic disadvantage** of going to the Emergency Department for non-emergencies, when the same conditions could be treated in my office or in an urgent care facility at a far lesser cost.

I informed her that if the cost of healthcare continued to escalate because of irresponsible utilization by the beneficiaries, that she might be one of those likely to be affected since she was young and of working age. This addressed her **'self-interest'** rather than her **'selfish interest'** and caught her attention.

I also pointed out to her that as a participant with the Medicaid program that it was in my own interest to see that the cost of healthcare was controlled. **I reminded her that I was the sole provider for Medicaid patients for miles and miles around and if through my inability to control costs I was removed from the panel of providers, she would have to seek her care elsewhere**. This showed her that my own interest in addressing the problem went beyond my own selfish interest and this further made her receptive to the discussion.

I pointed out to her that it would be extremely difficult for her to find another doctor within a thirty-five miles radius of where she lived. I knew that transportation would also be a problem for her. These issues further addressed both **her self-interest and my own self-interest.**

I then explained that there were numerous patients in the community who were without medical insurance, simply because the cost for healthcare was so high, and that the State of Michigan simply could not afford to provide them with medical coverage.

If as was projected, the cost of healthcare continued to rise unabated, many more individuals and families were likely to lose their coverage and these could include her other family members and even her children. This part of the discussion addressed the larger aspect or the **enlarged interest**.

I also pointed out to her that the cost of healthcare was funded by income taxes and even though she felt that this would not affect her, that other benefits to her would likely be diminished. She began to understand this also. This further addressed the **enlarged** interest.

I proceeded to show Annie that if she worked with me and cooperated in showing more responsible behavior, and if she were to encourage other friends and family to show the same type of responsible behavior we could help to control the cost of medical care and assist in saving the Medicaid program. By pointing this out to her we were now addressing the issue of **'enlightened interest.'** This further grabbed her attention.

I next showed her that if she were to modify her behavior as I suggested, **she could continue to have medical coverage**, she could continue to see me **and I would be able to continue to be her caregiver**. Since this was what we both wanted we had arrived at the point of **aligned interests**. Finding a solution from this point on was extremely simple.

We were now able to see the solution, which was that she would only use the Emergency Department for true emergencies and I would continue to be her physician. *I am proud to state that Annie is now one of my most 'compliant' patients.*

This in a simple form is an example of how the 'walk in the woods' is conducted.

They just flew two planes into my personal Twin Towers.

The biggest crisis that the USA and the world have probably faced in recent times was the destruction of the world trade center buildings, when fanatical terrorists flew two planes into the buildings.

Our reaction and that of the majority of the rest of the world was one of horror, sadness, anger and outrage at the sheer barbarism of the action. Our initial reaction was to immediately wish to totally annihilate every terrorist organization on the face of the earth. I must confess that this was also my initial reaction. **Even men of the cloth (religious people) were heard to utter similar sentiments.** This was a quite natural and acceptable reaction. The sheer enormity and barbarism of the action justified these feelings.

But our actual response and the response of President Bush were different and more measured. In retrospect, the response of President Bush and the government of the USA was a rational and justified response and obviously well thought out.

We first buried our dead, went through our period of mourning, carefully made our plans. We offered the Taliban government of Afghanistan the opportunity to turn over the terrorists. We waited patiently and when no response was forthcoming from the Taliban government, we took appropriate and justified action. The end result is public knowledge.

Similar situations of lesser severity develop everyday to everyone at some time or the other. When this happens, it is as if someone has taken planes and flown them into our personal twin towers.

An incident of a similar nature happened to me recently, which made me feel as if terrorists had flown two planes into my personal twin towers. The anger, disgust, frustration and desire to destroy the 'terrorists' who had 'attacked' me were identical to the general reaction of the population to the events of September 11th. My original reaction was a resolve to inflict maximum pain to those who had attacked my twin towers.

The incident that triggered this extreme reaction in me was a situation where I had reason to believe that the individual whom I shall call X, and with whom I was doing business had tried to defraud me of several thousand dollars.

The reason I felt so violated was because I had put in maximum effort to achieve success. I was so angered that for one entire day, I could not focus on anything. I knew that I had the capacity to inflict extreme pain (not actual physical pain) on the offending parties.

But I recognized this attitude went contrary to my professed beliefs that I have the power to teach anyone why and how to change their negative behavior. Yet here I was, so upset that I was planning to take action that was contrary to my newfound philosophy. I knew that force never yields meaningful change.

But how was I going to go about converting someone whose actions were ingrained in certain fixed attitudes and assumptions? For an entire night I couldn't sleep. I was torn between following my base instincts on one hand and adhering to the principles that I have been teaching others on the other hand. I knew that somehow I had lost control of the situation and I desperately needed to regain control.

By the next morning, I had regained some degree of control of the situation and I was determined not to deviate from my philosophy of meaningful change. I was allowing myself to lose control when I needed to assume control of the situation and basically direct my own future. I knew that I had the knowledge, skill and the capacity to achieve the results that I desired.

I prepared several options for the offending party to consider before deciding what my subsequent course of action would be. I was going to use every resource that I had at my disposal to encourage the offending party to make meaningful change rather than forcing change.

I sat down at my computer and prepared a letter that I could take to individual X's superior outlining the problem that I was having with individual X. I knew full well that this individual would not want the matter taken to a higher level. Another alternative would be to consult a lawyer as my family was encouraging me to do. To me both of these options would be to force change in the individual and I have stated repeatedly that forcing others to change is not meaningful.

If it ever became necessary to proceed with this course of action, I knew that there would be one winner and there would be one loser. But no matter who emerged winner, we would both lose something.

So before I took the letter to his superiors, I invited the individual in question to a meeting and insisted that she understand what the alternatives would be if she did not seek to solve the problem. I was very clear in pointing out to her that it was not my intention to be confrontational and I was very clear in pointing out to her that if we could each understand the other party's position that we would both stand to gain. I was very firm in suggesting we meet and I was determined to retain control of the situation .

Knowledge and understanding of the process of change puts the recipient of that knowledge in control at all times and the feeling of power is indescribable. During the subsequent meeting with individual X, I employed the 'walk in the woods' technique.

We went through the process, following each step before finally arriving at the point of aligned interests on our way to find a solution. I was finally able to convince the individual that we could both gain tremendously if we treated each other fairly and worked in a collaborative manner. Neither of us had to lose for the other to be a winner.

She was finally able to see where I was coming from and we came to an amicable arrangement. We shook hands and parted with the agreement that we would continue to work fairly with each other. I was satisfied with the outcome of the meeting.

But the most important lesson for me was the realization that no matter what, even after someone has flown planes into our personal twin towers we can still teach the offenders how to effect meaningful change.

The difference between the attack on my personal twin tower and the real towers of September 11th in New York is that no one died in the attack on my personal towers.

Therefore the response has to be commensurate with the severity of the atrocity perpetuated. I believe that in the September 11th incident, our government and the rest of the world took the appropriate action. Any other response would only result in a repetition of the same type of incidents by the offenders.

Sometimes we have to stop turning the other cheek. But I do believe that as much as possible we should help others who offend us to understand why a less confrontational attitude would yield greater benefits and we could all emerge as winners.

**With meaningful change,
there are no losers**

CHAPTER 9

Quality Improvement And The Need For Change

The Tiger Woods Effect

No, I do not have to lift weights.
No, I do not have to rebuild my swing.
No, I do not have to practice at night,
Unless I want to beat Tiger Woods
Tiger Woods
'Nike Advertisement'

This chapter is dedicated to those who play the game of golf since they more than anyone else would probably be better able to appreciate this section. **In addition I knew that I had to write a section for all my golfing buddies especially the ones from Carson City who go to Myrtle Beach every year, and the ones who go to Garland every year, so that they too could apply the process of change in order to improve their game.**

However the lessons to be learnt from this section are as applicable to those who understand and play golf, as it would be to those who like fishing or horse racing or making quilts. *I do confess that during some of my rounds of golf, some of these 'friends' have told me that I would have been better off fishing, especially when I was trying to retrieve balls from the water.*

As someone who plays golf (a duffer in golf terms) I cannot wait until the next golf season to see how much I have improved from the previous season.

I make changes to improve my golf swing. I buy new clubs. I experiment with new golf balls that are supposed to increase my driving distance or cure my slice. I read the Golf Digest magazines and learn how to reduce my score from 100's to 90's to 80's.

Of course I never accomplish these feats but I don't cease trying to change. **And above all, I imagine that I am Tiger Woods, hitting that perfect shot from out of a fairway bunker, over water to the green two hundred and ten yards away. Of course we all know where the ball ends up; in the water of course.** I suspect that there are a lot of others out there like me but they are not honest about it. Stand up and be counted if you are like me!

The reason we go out year after year constantly embarrassing ourselves is because we believe that we can improve through change and sometimes we succeed in hitting that perfect shot and we really believe that we should quit our jobs and go out and challenge and compete against Tiger Woods.

But enough about us duffers and hackers! The real story here is the effect that Tiger Woods has had on the game of golf and his fellow professionals and how we in turn can understand how the realization of the need to effect meaningful change can result in improved quality.

Before Tiger, there was the Golden Bear (Jack Nicklaus). Jack had set a standard in golf that few felt would ever be matched. We assumed that Jack Nicklaus had set the ultimate standard in golf. In an earlier section of the book, I stated that fixed assumptions are self-limiting and will eventually be proved false.

Well, along comes a young feller named Tiger Woods. Nobody ever told Tiger that the records that Jack Nicklaus set should not be broken. Moreover, Tiger never for one moment ever lived with the assumption that any of these records were beyond his ability.

Tiger clearly has no assumptions whatsoever about his abilities. Someone should have told this young man the realities of life because he soon begins to demolish all of Jack Nicklaus' records one after another. He wins the Masters tournament in 1997 by the obscene margin of 18 strokes. Even the great Jack Nicklaus says that Tiger is playing a game with which he (Jack) is not familiar. Pretty soon, the prevailing assumption is that Tiger would have no competition for years to come. This is another fixed assumption that we ought to discard.

While the rest of the world and his fellow golfers think that Tiger has peaked, Tiger on the other hand does not subscribe to our theory that he is incapable of improving. After winning his first Master's tournament by the obscene and embarrassing (for his opponents) eighteen strokes, he proceeds to break down his swing completely. The result is that the next year he fails miserably (by his own and the media standards).

The next year however, he proceeds to entertain us with what some describe as the greatest year in golf. Well, guess what? If Tiger Woods continues to demonstrate the same type of mental attitude as he did after the 1997 Masters tournament, I predict that "We ain't seen nothing yet!"

In the meantime world-class golfers of the caliber of David Duval, Ernie Els, Phil Mickelson, Vijay Singh, Colin Montgomerie, Sergio Garcia and countless others, begin to doubt themselves and their ability to compete with Tiger.

The biggest obstacle to these very talented and fine golfers being able to go on to the next level of their career lies in the fact that while Tiger Woods is competing **against** himself, and no one else, every other golfer is competing against themselves, the course and Tiger Woods. On the final day of a PGA tournament, every other golfer, rather than focusing on where they want to or can go, is looking back over his shoulder to see where Tiger is lying, in relation to the leader-board.

Pretty soon, these other golfers realized that if they were going to remain on tour and not continue to play second fiddle to Tiger, **they needed to change everything about their game, (their thoughts, their attitude, their swings, their work habits and their practice habits etc.)**

Out of the blue, these players and others like David Toms, Angel Cabrera, Thomas Bjorn, Mike Weir, Retief Goosen and even the previously unknown Jose Coceres emerge and start to win games in competition against Tiger Woods. Even the ancient **(by golf standards) Mark O'Meara, Tiger's buddy wins two majors in one year. Still, in spite of all this, Tiger remains head and shoulder above the rest of the field.**

The problem and the stumbling block for the other golfers is that while they are using Tiger as their benchmark, Tiger himself has set higher goals for himself. Therefore, while they are playing catch-up, Tiger is aiming at standards beyond what he has already set.

Until the other golfers cease to focus on Tiger Woods and dream their own dreams that would take them to the maximal limits of **their** potential, they would have as much chance as a snow cone in hell of exceeding Tiger Woods.

This is the effect that the realization of the need to change, followed by the desire to change and then implementing change can have on quality improvement. But for the other golfers to be able to maximize their potential and to have a fair chance of winning major tournaments, their dreams must exceed Tiger's.

Of course we must realize that for Tiger to remain at the top of his game, he himself has to continuously pursue change. If he did not, he would then enter a state of decline and the consequence of this would be decay in his game. But Tiger being a smart young man is not looking over his shoulder like the other golfers.

He recognizes that **his future lies in his own hands**. He recognizes that he and he alone will guide himself towards his ultimate goal. *That is why Tiger Woods has come from behind by as much as eight to nine strokes to win major tournaments on the final day.* While Tiger is inventing his own future, the other golfers are looking over their shoulders, wondering where Tiger is positioned on the leader board.

While Tiger Woods is competing against himself and inventing his own future, the other golfers are competing against **themselves and Tiger Woods. Instead of one opponent, they now have two of the most formidable opponents, their own anxiety and the colossal Tiger Woods.**

The end result therefore is that when this immensely talented group of golfers should be focused on inventing their own future, their focus is on a future of which Tiger Woods is the architect.

It is no coincidence that the immensely talented David Duval won his first major tournament only after he and Tiger Woods became good buddies.

It is also no coincidence that the only other player to win multiple majors in the same year is a forty plus year old guy named Mark O'Meara, who also happens to be Tiger's best buddy. Both David Duval and Mark O'Meara were able to elevate their games because the dreams that they were now able to dream were the expanded dreams that being close friends with Tiger allowed them to dream; whereas previously they were limited by their own limited dreams. Did Mark O'Meara suddenly and miraculously become a great golfer overnight? I don't think so. Therefore, one solution for all the other golfers is to become good buddies with Tiger. But Tiger has his own plans, so forget about that idea.

To get to the next level, every golfer must learn to project their dream beyond that of Tiger's and as long as they possess the talent, they would be able to achieve their goals. This is what I refer to as Tiger Woods effect on quality and the Tiger Woods effect on change.

I have purposely chosen Tiger Woods because at the time of writing this book, he is the most identifiable sports figure and one of the most easily identifiable figures worldwide. He also is one of the most identifiable figures of the present century and his mental model is consistent with the philosophy of meaningful change.

He also has set the standard by which we can define quality. Michael Jordan has done the same in basketball and Wayne Gretzky has done the same in hockey. **But when I look at how change affects quality, I choose to look to Tiger Woods.**

Quality is very hard to define. So often we hear of organizations pledging to provide better quality service. What is the definition of quality? Can we really adequately define quality? How do others define quality?

How does anyone define quality?

As one past Justice of the Supreme Court stated (when asked to adjudicate in a pornography case), **"I do not know how to define pornography but I know what it is when I see it.**

When I look at Tiger, I know that he represents the ultimate in quality when I see him in action. **Quality is what the competition is always trying to emulate**. So I find it interesting that Tiger recognizes intuitively, that in order for him to stay ahead of the competition, he too must continue to change himself.

When Mark McGuire broke Roger Maris' record, it took almost 25 years to accom-

plish this feat. Mark felt, as did many others that his record would stand at least as long as Maris' record. Yet in less than 3 years, Barry Bond has broken the record of McGuire and Sammy Sosa broke Maris' record in three successive years.

What these examples demonstrate is that **when we change our mental model, we can accomplish as much as we dream. Quality improvement requires that we must recognize the constant need to visualize change and we must constantly seek out change and implement change but whatever change we make must be meaningful change.**

Tiger Woods' mental model is such that he believes that he can demolish all of Jack Nicklaus' records. The standards that Tiger in turn has set, has forced all the other professional golfers on the PGA tour to retool their mental models. **Tiger Woods has created a crisis in the professional lives of the other golfers on the PGA tour. Their livelihood and their reputation in history are at stake.**

As I have said repeatedly in this book, **crisis forces change**, but change that is forced on others is not usually meaningful. For change to be meaningful, these golfers need to change their mental model.

The depressing fact for these golfers must be the realization that Tiger Woods is far from having reached his peak! **I hope for Tiger's sake that no one seeks to hire the goons that Tonya Harding's husband hired to injure Nancy Kerrigan!**

The exciting part is that some young gun out there will emerge with a mental model that tells him that he can exceed Tiger's capabilities and Tiger will need to constantly seek out change to stay ahead of the competition.

Even as I write this book a young man by the name of **Ty Tryon** has emerged to challenge Tiger for his crown. It remains to be seen whether he has the same mental model as Tiger. **Whatever the outcome the future looks great for golf!**

We see the same effect in other professional sports such as basketball, football and hockey and any other sport.

Does anyone truly believe that no one is going to come along to challenge the accomplishments of Michael Jordan or Walter Payton or Wayne Gretzky? **How could we continue to hold fixed assumptions about anything in sport when there are players like Kobe Bryant, Grant Hill, Tracy Mc Grady, Vince Carter or Shane Battier in basketball and how can we seriously think that they lack the talent of Michael Jordan? The question is do they have the mental model of Michael Jordan?**

Or how about Marshall Faulk or Eddie George or Kurt Warner or Ricky Williams in football? Or how about that kid who is now sharpening his skates and polishing his hockey skills on some frozen lake in Uzbekistan or some other previously unheard of part of the world?

After all in the United States, home of basketball, there are now professional basketball players from Yugoslavia and Turkey. "Where? Who?" you ask.

Didn't the Toronto Blue Jays win the World Series in baseball? **Twice! Didn't anyone tell those Canadians that baseball was an American monopoly?** And how about the United States hockey teams winning the Stanley Cup by beating Canadian teams? "Absolutely unheard of!" You say; but only if you were holed up in some cave in Afghanistan for thirty years or so.

Physicians, as a group, have a reputation for being lovers of golf. Every year these physicians recognize the need and seek to make changes in their golf game in the hopes of improvement. **Yet physicians as a group have a reputation, more than any other group for being most resistant to change in their profession**.

In addition, they have a reputation for being more resistant to change when compared with any other professional groups. I say this as a member of this group and as one who has been as guilty as anyone else in the past, of being resistant to change.

It amazes me to realize that in my profession, so many of my colleagues feel that they are doing the best job possible and do not see a need for change. **Many of these people have been practicing medicine in the same way as they have done, for as long as 30 years or more.**

They have not changed the style or content of their practice in 30 years and yet they feel that they are providing the highest possible standard of care.

But why am I picking on physicians? Are physicians the only ones resistant to change? Absolutely not! As I have stated previously, the same principles and philosophy regarding the process of change are as applicable in any other sphere of our lives, whether as individuals, in our relationships, in our businesses and organizations or in our society. **Resistance to change is not unique to physicians. This is a universal problem.**

Instead of using the Tiger Woods analogy, we can substitute any successful organization or individual or institution or relationship. The lesson remains the same. **Before we can seek improvement in quality, we must perceive the need to change, we must desire to change and then we must plan and implement meaningful change.**

It is educational to see the large numbers of people who go on the golf courses year after year, hitting ball after ball but seeing no improvement in their scores. These individuals usually subscribe to every golf magazine, every golf instructional video, every new driver which promises twenty extra yards to their drives and they go out day after day trying to hit the ball 300 yards like Tiger Woods.

Usually they succeed in gaining a few extra yards on their drives; **assuming they can find the ball in the woods or can retrieve it from the water. (Incidentally, they are** easily identified by the high technical quality of their ball-retrievers and I recognize them instantly when they present to my office for treatment of poison ivy from searching for their balls in the woods!)

Their scores however do not improve. The reason? They fail to implement meaningful change in their games and so they fail to attain their objective, which is to improve their scores. *On the other hand, I am proud to say that some of my best friends (whose names shall be withheld to protect the guilty) have improved their scores significantly in the past few years; their beer drinking scores that is. Smile guys. You know who you are. Cheers! I would give you credit by mentioning your names but I am not sure that your wives would ever let you back on the golf course and I need playing partners.*

Unlike those golfers who are obsessed with hitting the three hundred and fifty yard drives **(with a hurricane wind behind their back, downhill and on rock hard ground)**, those individuals who go out and practice putting and chipping **(the short game)** continue to see improvement in their scores.

It was instructive to read in Tiger Woods' book **"How I play Golf"** a comment that Tiger makes regarding putting. In the words of the greatest golfer currently, the great Tiger Woods himself, **"There is always room for improvement."**

When I examine the lives and careers of great individuals and great companies and organizations, the one factor that stands out is **the recognition by these great ones of the need for constant work at improvement and they instinctively know how to improve and succeed. This is the willingness to embrace and make <u>meaningful</u> change.**

Michael Jordan, Tiger Woods, Jack and Arnie, John Elway, Bill Gates, Jack Welch, Coca-Cola, IBM and countless others understood instinctively the need for **<u>meaningful</u>** change to keep ahead of the competition. They embraced change.

McDonald's Restaurant started selling burritos and tacos when they realized that Burger King and Wendy's had learnt how to make good hamburgers too. Even Wal-Mart which once proudly boasted, "We only sell American made products," recognized the need for change.

I mentioned in an earlier section of the book that Coca-Cola once tried resurrecting the original coke bottle when their sales were flagging. The experiment was **a successful flop**. The question is, "Was this meaningful change?" If the result of this change was a revitalization and growth of the company, then it would indeed be meaningful. If not it is pure window-dressing. These type of changes are cosmetic changes.

The fact that many of the great achievers understood instinctively about the need for change does not mean that they understand the process of change. This explains why many of them succeed in one area but fail miserably later or in other areas of endeavor.

This failure to grasp the principles of change or to understand the process of change also explains why many great sportsmen retire and then return to the game only to face ignominious failure when they return.

It is therefore a critical factor of change that everyone needs to understand the process of change. **Michael Jordan knew instinctively what he needed to do to improve his game as a basketball player. Yet when he tried baseball and golf, he failed**.

Failure to understand the process of change also explains "Peter's Principle", which is that given the opportunity, everyone will eventually rise to his/her level of incompetence.

The purpose of this book is to teach others that each one of us can learn the techniques that the great ones and great companies and great organizations understood instinctively and to apply the same principles in our daily lives, in our relationships, in our business practices and organizations and in our societies.

No this book will not make some of you duffers into Tiger Woods, nor will it make any of you weekend warriors into Michael Jordan or John Elway; not unless you have similar talents to these great athletes and you are prepared to work as hard as they did.

Neither will it make any of you computer nerds into Bill Gates or Paul Allen. After all we do not all have similar talents. Moreover these individuals started developing their individual talents at an early age. This explains why Michael Jordan failed at baseball and did not succeed in emulating Tiger Woods in golf.

What this book could do is it could allow those individuals with equal talent as others to achieve similar levels of success. **In other words, the Detroit Lions can achieve the same level of success as the Dallas Cowboys but the Valley Lutheran Chargers would not.**

Who would challenge the fact that David Duval, Phil Mickelson, Sergio Garcia and a host of other golfers have similar talent as Tiger Woods? The question then is why have they not achieved the same level of success as Tiger?

Phil Mickelson, one of the most talented golfers has yet to win a major golf tournament. The reason must be that Phil in spite of his great skills is unable to recognize what it takes to effect meaningful change and has consequently failed to effect the type of change necessary to take him over the top. It is not too late for Phil Mickelson to recognize the need for meaningful change and to make those necessary changes to win his first major tournament this year.

No, this book will not make you an Olympic champion. **You will do that yourself**

providing that you have the talent and the time to put in the effort. What this book will do is to guide you and everyone else and allow everyone the opportunity to visualize the benefits of change, to understand the process of change and to continually strive to improve by making **meaningful** change and to strive towards achieving their **maximal potential.**

I happened to read Tiger Woods' book titled "How I play golf". I thought it was a wonderful, well-written book. It was full of "How toes". There was "How to smoke the driver", and "How to get it down". There was "How to putt" and "How to escape from the sand". There was even a chapter on "How to master the mind". In fact, every chapter was a "How to".

I pictured the many people reading that book and going out to the driving range trying everything that Tiger suggested in his book. I pictured the once a week golfers, imagining themselves accomplishing Tiger Woods' magnificent feats. **I also pictured these individuals becoming frustrated when they continued to hit balls into the water or into the woods (not a pun!)**

And I realized that there was one chapter that was not included in Tiger's book and which would have made the most significant difference in the readers' games. And that would have been a chapter on **"How to effect meaningful change, in your own game"**. Because, whether you like it or not, we do not all possess the same talents as Tiger Woods, or Wayne Gretzky or Michael Jordan, or John Elway, or Bill Gates for that matter.

These same principles of change are applicable whether we are selling hamburgers or manufacturing and selling motorcars or computers.

These same principles of change are equally applicable in personal relationships, in health care, in organizations and in society. When relationships fail, or organizations fail, it is because individuals do not recognize the need to make **meaningful** change or are unable to visualize mechanisms to effect meaningful change or are afraid to implement change.

So you ask, "What relevance does Tiger Woods and golf have to you or your institution?" In my own institution, as in every hospital in the United States, we are subject to annual inspections by JCAHO (The Joint Commission on Accreditation of Hospitals.) This is a government-funded organization whose responsibility is to inspect all hospitals in the country to ensure that **minimum** standards are met.

Every year when the time arrives for JCAHO inspection, everyone in the hospital runs around like chickens with their heads cut off, trying to ensure that we are JCAHO compliant. One recurrent complaint can be heard every year **after** the JCAHO inspections. That is, *"how come we failed to meet JCAHO standards when we passed with flying colors last year and we haven't changed a thing? Those JCAHO people are* *not consistent. I think someone in JCAHO had it in for us." This is precisely the point I make when I say that we need to constantly seek and make meaningful change.*

The point that is missed is that JCAHO **doesn't care whether we are doing the same things** as we did last year. As far as JCAHO is concerned, **if we made no change from last year, then we have made no improvement and as the diagram in Figure 1 shows, if no change has occurred, then chances are that our quality has decreased and JCAHO is about quality improvement,** *not maintaining the status quo.*

Therefore if we are to ensure that we pass JCAHO inspections every year, with flying colors, we must seek *not to meet the minimum standards set by JCAHO but we must look into the future and set the goals that we feel that we can achieve and exceed JCAHO standards.* **Other wise JCAHO will judge us by 'Tiger Woods' standards and if we have not come any closer to those standards compared to the year previously, then we would have failed to meet standards of quality care.**

Every institution needs to recognize this fact before their next JCAHO inspections are due. I have tried to suggest to some of my colleagues that our institution should aspire not to be the next Mayo Clinic, but greater than the Mayo Clinic. Unless we can dream great and aspire to the highest ideals, then we will constantly be trying to play catch up like the other golfers chasing Tiger Woods. Or, if not, when we face competition by another group or institution, we will constantly have to be looking back over our shoulder to see where the competition lies and even if we have an eight-stroke lead over our competition they will soon catch up with us and beat us in the playoffs.

We can learn many lessons from Tiger Woods and we can all apply these principles in our lives and in our institutions and make the necessary meaningful type of change that would allow us to grow.

Through meaningful change we could all reach our maximal potential and this is translated into improved quality.

CHAPTER 10

The Futurist And Change

The great hockey player does not go to where the puck is.
He goes to where he anticipates the puck will be.
Wayne Gretzky.

What is a futurist? **A futurist is someone who anticipates the future before it has happened and visualizes the need for change before it occurs.**

We all of us need to become futurists. We have the **capacity to change the future if we can visualize the future, as we would like it to be**. Of course we can never anticipate the unexpected. The unexpected is often the result of our inability to anticipate and plan for the future.

You may well ask how can anyone visualize the future. **No one can visualize the precise future, not even Nostradamus**. But we can all visualize the future; as we would like it to be. If we can visualize the future as we would **like** it to be, we can then plan and make the necessary adjustments to allow such a future to happen. *We can alter the course of our future if we can visualize what we would like our future to be and plan for this to happen.*

In business this is referred to as strategic planning. I dislike this term immensely because it fails to convey the message of meaningful change. Besides, if strategic planning is the answer to meaningful change, how is it that so many successful businessmen absolutely fail in their personal endeavors and in personal relationships.

I can name numerous instances of individuals who are excellent strategic planners and haven't got a clue about how to make those meaningful changes that would have allowed them to preserve their marriages. You the reader know who those individuals are, so I do not need to name them. They are to be found in every village, every town and every city. As they say in the business, pick your poison. The purpose of this book is not about embarrassing people but about helping people.

I therefore encourage you to abandon the term strategic planning and encourage you to use the term "Meaningful Change" and to think in these terms. I assure you that your successes will be greater when you think in these terms.

In order to help people in their quest for meaningful change, I teach them about the six basic steps in the process of change and I employ what I call my **"magical mirror experiment"** to take them through the six-step process. I have devoted an entire chapter to teach the principles of the "magical mirror experiment." My **magical mirror experience** is a modification of what Peter Drucker of the Drucker Foundation refers to as **the mirror test. I have modified the technique to change it from a test to make it into an experience, which changes the person looking into the mirror instantly**. The change is instant and dramatic and that is why I call it my magical mirror experiment.

I have yet to find a single individual that has not been instantly changed as a result of the mirror experience. The mirror experience is a fundamental and vital component in teaching people the process of change.

I encourage everyone who wishes to learn how to effect meaningful change to learn the technique of conducting the experiment and to practice it daily. Invest some time in this activity and I assure you that the return on your investment will be well worth the effort.

I learnt to become a futurist and to think like a futurist because of Lee Kaiser, who, as I stated previously in another section of this book, is one of the greatest philosophers I have ever encountered. Lee Kaiser opened my eyes to "futurism".

Futurism requires that we cast aside all our fixed assumptions. We also need to constantly re-examine previous assumptions and be prepared to challenge every single assumption about any and everything that we were ever taught. This is how we release ourselves from our bubble.

Futurism offers **hope** for the future. If we can project the future, **as we would like it to be**, then there is hope in our lives. Futurism allows us to see the light at the end of the tunnel. **Futurism allows us to see the oasis when we have been wandering in the desert. Futurism is the cure for depression and anxiety**.

Depression and despair come about when individuals or societies cannot see any hope for meaningful change. Hope can only come about as a result of our ability to visualize a future, as we would like it to be and to believe that such a future is possible to achieve.

Since September 11th, numerous articles have been written about the future of airport security and the use of retinal scans and computer generated digital photographic profiles for identifying passengers. Techniques for scanning passengers' luggage for bombs will be enhanced. These are examples of meaningful change, not taking away toothpicks and nail clippers from passengers.

Recently there was a report about a surgical procedure that was performed by a surgical team four thousand miles away from where the patient was located. This might seem amazing at this time. But I predict that in the not too distant future that this type of surgery will become the norm rather than the exception. Surgeons on earth will be able to perform emergency operations on people in space.

Today I can communicate with someone at the far end of the earth and have a visual image and real time conversations with that person by means of my computer. **In the future I will be able to project my thoughts directly onto a computer screen and I would be able to save myself the traumatic experience of getting carpal tunnel syndrome from endless hours of typing.** Just a few years ago, this was considered stuff for Disney World!

So many changes have taken place in our world and so many changes are occurring that it literally boggles the mind. We can go as far as our dreams can take us. Just picture all the changes that have taken place just in our lifetime. Everywhere around us we can see examples of meaningful change, from the microwave to cellular telephones. Without these changes, our growth would have been stagnant.

Yet when I make the prediction to my colleagues and my own family that the hospital of the future will be a hospital without walls, they think I am a stark raving lunatic. "Where," my son asks, "will they treat trauma victims?" "Where," my colleagues ask, "will they perform major surgeries?"

Well! I answer, "Do you remember how we treated Tuberculosis twenty-five years ago?" "Can you remember how long patients remained in hospitals after gallbladder operations, just fifteen years ago?"

Once upon a time, according to ancient lore, patients who developed TB, were confined to TB hospitals, called sanatoriums and were made to stay there, away from their families for six months. Those hospitals are now as extinct as the Roman Empire.

Once upon a time the story continues, when patients had gallbladder surgeries, they were confined to hospital beds for three weeks. I know this because I was a general surgeon before I decided to make the switch to Family Practice. Today, patients who have gallbladder operations are sent home within twenty-four hours. **This is a vast improvement in the quality of care and yet physicians and patients complain that the HMOs are forcing the patients to go home too soon.**

Hospitals are for sick people. Why on earth would anyone want to stay in a hospital? Hospitals carry all kinds of dangerous germs. I would think that anyone in his/her right senses would want to avoid staying in hospitals just as much as they would like to avoid smallpox.

Yet there are among us, colleagues who bemoan the shorter hospital stays that managed care has imposed on our patients: **this despite the fact that outcomes are better!** Complication rates are minimized when we are able to get patients home in a shorter period of time. The same thing applies to open-heart surgeries and total hip replacement surgeries.

I recall a football player from the Cincinnati Bengals football team, (Ickey Woods, no relation to Tiger), returning to play with the team within two weeks of having hernia surgery. This was virtually unheard of before his time. Jack Nicklaus returned to playing professional golf within weeks of having a Total Hip Replacement operation.

I had a discussion with a senior colleague recently over lunch, when his wife was hospitalized. He bemoaned the fact that because of the HMOs, his wife was only going to be allowed to remain in hospital for five days.

He bemoaned the fact that his daughter-in-law, who had recently had a baby, was only allowed to remain in hospital for two days. When I suggested that she could easily have gone home in one day, he looked at me in such a way that I seriously thought that he was giving serious thought to ending my life.

I hastily mentioned the examples discussed above and informed him that my own mother had delivered thirteen children at home without a single complication. As I hastily attempted to soothe his anger towards me, I reconsidered the fact and concluded that maybe one of her children had indeed suffered brain damage at birth and that it was I!

And so I say to my doubting son and my doubting colleagues; the hospital of the future will be a hospital without walls! I predict that in the future, when patients require major surgeries **(if they still do)**; that a vehicle, similar to the virtually extinct ice-cream vans, will pull up at the patients' homes.

The patients will be brought out to the waiting vehicle and the surgery will be performed in the driveway and the patient will re-enter her/his home immediately. Care will then be continued in the home by a team of visiting nurses and various therapists and the outcomes will be much better than when patients were confined within the walls of hospitals for similar problems.

My good friend and colleague Dr. Hugh Holder, for the past ten years, has been practicing a style of medicine that is now considered novel and revolutionary in the United States and this is generating great excitement in the medical community.

For the past ten years, Hugh has been providing Total In-Home Care. This is not house call. He has been treating patients with a multitude of medical problems completely in their home. These are patients who previously would have required hospitalization and who in many other places still do.

This type of care is generating great interest in the medical community and will constitute the new standard of quality care in the future. **Yet when my friend approached**

Blue Cross and Blue Shield about looking into his recommendations, he wasn't given the time of day. I hope that I can avoid any further encounters with my senior colleague who I mentioned earlier if and when he hears of my future predictions about healthcare!

Twenty years ago when I was a practicing surgeon in Barbados, I performed surgeries on tourists who needed it, returned them to their hotels and provided care for them in their hotels. Many of these patients, even though they were not able to enjoy going into the water, could at least sit on the beach and enjoy the sea, sun and sand. Both they and their families appreciated what I was doing for them since the families did not need to interrupt their vacation making hospital visits. The insurance companies also benefited from the reduced cost. And the tourist industry benefited since tourists didn't need to worry that their vacations would be spoilt if they became ill.

I was thinking like a futurist even before I knew what the concept of futurism was all about. I was a futurist without knowing that I was one. **Now that I think about it, I wish to retract the statement that I learnt to become a futurist from the eminent Lee Kaiser. Maybe he heard about me first. Nevertheless there is no finer person to learn about how to become a futurist than Lee Kaiser.**

This then is how a futurist thinks! If we can predict the future and anticipate and plan for change, then we can avoid the shock that will befall us **when change is forced upon us**. Healthcare and many other industries are in crisis and heading for chaos. We can avoid the chaos that will follow if we start planning and seeking to implement meaningful change. The situation is identical in virtually every organization and industry in this and every other country.

As a futurist, my objective is to try to predict the future, plan for it and seek to live in it. Anyone who can anticipate the future is likely to be several steps ahead of those individuals who can only wait for the future to fall around their ears.

Their reaction will predictably be like that of Chicken Little, "The sky is falling! The sky is falling!" And they would then be late in reacting to change.

The future offers great hope and promise as I visualize it. I only use the past to help me predict the future. **Too many people live in the past and lack the ability to visualize the future, as they would like it to happen**. This is sad, because so many of these individuals are consumed by the bitterness of past experiences and see no hope for change in the future.

Anyone can become a futurist. We simply need to start thinking and acting like futurists. There is a simple game that you can play with your friends to help you think like and to become a futurist.

Challenge yourself or a friend to come up with the most outrageous ideas of significant developments in the future. The problem would be to justify your recommendation that this would be a feasible development. Here are some examples of futuristic ideas:

1. **In the future people in one country would purchase multi-million dollar homes in another country, just from seeing these homes on the Internet. Oops! That idea is already here.**
2. **Enron, the largest energy producer would file for bankruptcy. Shucks, that idea is already old news.**
3. **O.K, here's a good one. I could speak to my friend in Argentina and she and I can see each other simultaneously on our computers. No? Do you mean to tell me that idea is also old news?**
4. **Well, how about this one? In the United States, racism, bigotry and dis crimination will be eliminated. What do you mean that will never hap pen?**
5. **O.K. here's one that I am sure will work. The Detroit Lions will win the Super Bowl in 2004 and the Detroit Tigers baseball team will get to the World Series in the same year. Come on! What do you mean that only one of those things will happen?**

All right, I give up. How about some of your suggestions? How about noise less drills in the dentists' office, as my dentist Dr. Paul Koepke suggested. Remember that it is not necessary to confine the changes to technological developments but the suggestions can be expanded to any action that would result in significant changes in any aspect of society in any part of the world.

This game stimulates you to think like a futurist. The better you become at it this increases your **eligibility to run for the position of President of the United States.**

'When my older son graduated from college, he decided to set up his own business. He started an Internet business dealing with international luxury real estate. When he approached me with the idea and told me that he was going to limit the homes on his website to homes in excess of $2 million, I pooh-poohed the idea and told him to go and get a real job. At the time, my son was thinking like a futurist and I was not. Fortunately my son was not discouraged by me and went ahead with his idea.

When he approached the first realtor requesting some homes to be put on his website, he was brushed aside like a pesky fly. Through his persistence, he finally convinced a realtor in Florida to give his website a chance. The first home he placed on his website was worth in excess of $36 million and the 'house' came with a guest house which exceeded 6000 square feet. The next homes he put on his site were *from Hawaii and belonged to the producer of the TV show "Lifestyles of the rich and famous"*

By the time he had acquired several other multi-million dollar homes, the realtor who had originally rejected him was calling him and begging to have her homes placed with his site.

Today I encourage my children to continue to think like futurists. The world desperately needs more futurists. We need more meaningful change in our society.'

Invent your own future now!

> You see things and you say, "Why?"
> But I dream things that never were:
> and say "Why not?"

CHAPTER 11

This Is Not A Handicap, This Is An Opportunity

Give the man a fish vs. teaching him to fish.
'Give a man a fish and you will feed him for a day. Teach him how to fish and you will feed him for life.'
         Old Chinese Proverb

The tragedy of modern medicine is that we have been conditioned to believe that we can solve every problem with a pill. Unfortunately, patients have also been led to believe that this is so because they have never been offered alternative solutions and they in turn expect to be treated this way. **The tragedy of modern medicine is also the tragedy of modern society, which is that we expect quick fixes. But quick fixes are not always the most appropriate solutions to our problems.**

It may well be true that this is the way, as physicians, we were taught in medical school. But it is equally true that **it is also extremely convenient for us** to hand out pills to patients because it is more time-consuming to sit down with patients and to help them find real solutions to their problems.

Fast foods have certainly made it more convenient for people to grab a bite while on the run. But fast foods have also contributed to the increased incidence of obesity with all the additional consequences of diabetes and hypertension and heart disease in our society. I do not see that the fast food industry has made any type of meaningful change in our society. I can already see the day when Ralph Nader will lead the battle against the fast food industry just like the battle was joined against the tobacco industry.

Maybe someone in the fast food industry will come up with innovative foods that will serve the purpose of catering to the public's desire for fast food without contributing to the increased incidence of diabetes and heart disease. *'Subway' the maker of subway sandwiches has already recognized the need and is capitalizing on their famous low-fat chicken sandwiches. Subway Sandwiches are now sponsors of The American Heart Association heart walk.*

Until I recognized the need for meaningful change in my practice, I was just as guilty as any other physician of practicing quick fix medicine. When I changed my style of practice I recognized the dramatic and meaningful changes I was able to make in my patients lives and my eyes were truly opened.

It was a "WOW" experience, not only for me but also for my patients. These same patients who had been dependent on medication for many years, suddenly were able to liberate themselves from these noxious drugs. **I do not for one moment suggest that we can or should abandon use of medications.** *What I am suggesting is that we have abused the use of medication simply because we failed to grasp a simple concept of the need for meaningful change. The use of medications should and could be the last resort in many instances*

In our upside down world, the reverse holds true. The result is a tremendous economic burden on the national budget and that is why we need meaningful change. Inefficient use of resources is not confined to the medical profession and in fact runs across the board. It is simply easier for me as a physician to use the medical profession as an example. But as I have stated, you can take the same principles and apply them in any aspect of life

We have pills for virtually every disease known to man. There are pills for depression, generalized anxiety, social anxiety, social phobia, fibromyalgia, erectile dysfunction, ADHD, diabetes, hypertension, and high cholesterol. You name it and we've got it! We even treat viruses with antibiotics!

The net effect is that we have sent the cost of medical care skyrocketing. In addition we expose our patients to all the noxious side effects of these very potent drugs. **Doesn't the Hippocratic oath caution us about first doing "no harm"?**

Are we or are we not harming our patients when we practice inefficient medicine by giving them unnecessary medications and recommending unnecessary procedures for them.

I remember only too well when it was almost fashionable to remove children's tonsils and adenoids. **I remember when I was a practicing surgeon, having 300 patients on a waiting list for surgery for tonsil removal**. I remember only too well when removal of heel spurs was the bread and butter of podiatrists. These operations went down the same path as Tyrannosaurus Rex and Stegosaurus.

There was a time when it was also fashionable to remove women's uterus, until medical research told us that many of these operations were unnecessary. *Every day, millions of babies are made to endure the ritual of circumcision, in the name of 'personal hygiene,' and the pretext of preventing cancer of the penis, when all that is necessary is to teach the parent and child how to retract the foreskin while in the shower.*

119

We have taken a religious ritual and made it almost mandatory in the society. In some cases, parents have been encouraged to have their children circumcised, **'so that they can look like their friends and their brothers.'**

Why don't we recommend nose jobs on all our children? I would have certainly preferred a nose job compared to the alternative that is being offered. We can send all our children to the surgeon of some of our famous pop singers so that they can all, **'be like Mike,' the other Mike.**

One definition of 'Quality' states that it is, **'doing everything possible that needs to be done and not doing what does not need to be done!'** *When we provide pills that patients do not really need or are more likely to cause more harm than alternative solutions, we cannot possibly claim to be practicing good medicine, much less high quality medicine.*

We must change our mental model and we must help our patients to understand how to change **their** own mental models.

Anyone who does not see the need for meaningful change because of their own perceived selfish interests also fails to understand the theory of "inter-connectedness." *When the cost of medical care goes up, we are all affected both directly and indirectly*. The same managed care that we all oppose then becomes more intrusive and we find that crisis situations develop which force us to change.

Remember that **crisis forces us to change; but change that is brought on by crisis is usually a shock to our system and we often resent this. Remember that managed care evolved because of the inability of those in the medical field to anticipate, plan for and to implement change?**

Of course we can blame the lawyers for the current situation of medicine today! That would be an easy explanation for our problems and we would be absolved of all responsibility! But the fact of the matter is that when we adopt this position, we have not changed our mental model.

We have adopted the position that we are incapable of either changing ourselves or to be able to effect meaningful change in the system. Either way, we are contributing to our own demise. This situation leads to more anxiety and frustration and the net effect is that more and more physicians take an early retirement. **Someone please call Jack Kevorkian! We desperately need his help.**

When patients come in to our practices and request antibiotics for viral illnesses, it is because of a mental model that they have developed over the years, sometimes cultivated by us. If we can get our patients to change their mental model, we can avoid prescribing unnecessary and harmful antibiotics.

Let us examine other less obvious situations where we might be able to influence patients to change their mental models and avoid using these unnecessary and harmful drugs.

Recently, one of my patients came into my office stating that he was having difficulty sleeping. My first impression and as it turned out, the correct one, was the patient was experiencing anxiety related symptoms.

I then determined through enquiry that the patient had been married for fifteen years and the problem with his sleep had been ongoing for about 10 years. During this time, the patient and his wife were experiencing problems with his daughter from a previous marriage.

The patient loved his wife and desired to preserve his marriage but he also had a commitment to his daughter. For ten years, the patient had been prescribed sleeping pills by other physicians and had even seen counselors.

My initial inclination was to continue prescribing these ineffectual medications but instead I decided to apply the principles of change that I had been developing over time. Anxiety arises because of the feeling of lack of control and fear of uncertainty.

This patient felt that he had no control of the situation between his wife and his daughter and feared the consequence of trying to provide a solution. He desperately feared having to choose between the two people that he loved.

I reassured the patient that he did not have to worry about making choices but that he needed to learn how to implement meaningful change between his wife and his daughter and to show them how a collaborative relationship would be a better overall solution. I demonstrated my technique for effecting meaningful change and showed him how to apply the technique in his relationships with his wife and daughter.

I introduced the concept of the "mirror experiment" to him. I taught him how to negotiate change and how to use basic marketing skills to achieve buy-in to his ideas. I showed him the economic benefits of preserving his relationships with his wife and daughter and how he needed to and could improve the relationship between his wife and daughter. He carefully assimilated what I was trying to teach him and he began to grasp the principles of my lesson.

The effect on my patient was dramatic! Suddenly he felt that he had regained control of a situation where he previously felt that he had no control. Suddenly he realized that the underlying basis of his sleeping problem for the past ten years and all his anxiety was the result of his loss of control of the situation between he, his wife and daughter. **Regaining control of a situation where he had previously lost control eliminated his feelings of anxiety and his sleep habits improved.**

He did not want any sleeping pills anymore and I did not give him any. **Rather than give him a fish for a day, I taught him how to fish for the rest of his life**. I cannot describe the gratification that I felt that day and I cannot describe the gratitude of that patient.

This is not a handicap, this is an opportunity

Jimmie M was one of my first patients in private practice in Michigan. He had been in Law enforcement for 22 years until a motor vehicle accident resulted in an injury to his right hand. After four unsuccessful surgeries to try and correct the problem, it was decided that Jimmie would have to go on some type of disability.

However, the company for which he worked decided that they would help him find alternative employment and offered to train him in computers. In the meantime, his case had gone before a lawyer and attempts were being made to settle the case through arbitration.

Jimmie came to me with his arm in a cast and bitterly complained about how his company would not understand his handicap and how rather than allowing him to go on disability, they were trying to find alternative employment.

At first I was extremely sympathetic to Jimmie's plight but in the aftermath of what had happened on September 11th, I saw his problem as minor compared to what the victims and relatives were undergoing.

I looked him straight in the eye and holding out my right hand to mimic his, I stated quite firmly, **"This is not a handicap, this is an opportunity!"** I repeated the statement about three more times for effect.

I then showed Jimmie the diagram in Figure 1 and pointed out to him where he might have been on the evolutionary path of change had the injury not occurred to him. I pointed out to him that having been in the same field of Law enforcement for 23 years, that the possibility existed that very soon he would likely have become bored with his job. If that stage had arrived before his accident, he would likely have been stuck in a dead-end job for years to come.

I pointed out to him that the company was offering him an opportunity to explore other avenues. Chances were that he could find himself rising higher than he could ever have hoped to go had he remained in his original job.

I explained to him that change offers us the chance to grow and rather than looking at his injured arm as a handicap, that this should be looked upon as an opportunity for change and growth.

I used the analogy of the Twin Towers to show him that someone had flown two planes into his twin towers **(his arm)**. Crisis had developed and out of that crisis had emerged chaos and turmoil in his life with respect to his career. I told him the anecdote of the little boy and the blocks, which I related in an earlier section of the book.

As I pointed out to him, just like the little boy who had kicked down all the houses that he had built from his four hundred blocks, he could use the same creativity as the little boy used, to build a beautiful castle and use the opportunity to create a better future for himself, instead of the **'oh woe is me attitude'** that he had adopted.

I showed him how, just like our country that has the opportunity to stare down adversity and overcome it to go on to become better, he had the same opportunity to face his personal adversity and become ten times greater than he was before.

This strapping law enforcement officer broke down in tears and admitted that he had been using his injury as a crutch and admitted that he had not looked at his situation with the same degree of positivism as I had shown him. He left my office much happier than when he came to see me and before he left, he outlined to me several possible alternative careers that he could already seen in front of him.

I had taught another person to fish and not be dependent on handouts of fish for the rest of his life.

**Learning how to effect
meaningful change restores
control into your life.**

CHAPTER 12

Practical Applications Of The Doctrine Of Change

How can we apply the knowledge of how to effect meaningful change practically? How can we apply this knowledge to make a **real** difference in our lives? Having studied the process and understood why we should change, how we can change and how we can influence change in others, there are two questions that need to be answered, **"So what?"** and **"Now what?"**

We have discussed the statement that meaningful change only comes from changing the mental model and that meaningful change is vital to assure continued growth of the individual, personal relationships, companies, organizations, communities and whole societies.

We have also addressed the fact that changing the mental model is also necessary for continued growth of our spiritual being. **The secret of life lies in our ability to be continually reborn and continuous rebirth only comes from understanding how to effect meaningful change.**

We have discussed the six steps that we must all undergo in order to effect meaningful change. These steps are repeated in several sections throughout this book. To reiterate, the six steps are; (1) **recognizing** that change is a necessary fact of life, (2) **visualizing** the benefits of change in the future (and the consequences of **no change**), (3) **accepting** the need to change, (4) the willingness to change or **desiring** change, (5) developing a **plan** or mental map to follow and (6) following that map or **implementing** the plans.

Knowing how to effect <u>meaningful</u> change is a fundamental law of life!

Fundamental to understanding this fundamental law then is that **we must operate within an open mental model**. I cannot emphasize enough the fact that open mental models permit growth. **Closed mental models are essentially dead**.

Let us now look at some different situations where understanding the process of being able to effect meaningful change can be used practically.

Individuals

Using the graphics of the evolutionary path of change in Figure 1, it is clear that **every** individual has the potential to grow and every individual **can** grow. **Growth equals gain**. This gain can be economic, financial, physical or spiritual. We all can benefit from any of these types of gain. We may not all **desire** economic, financial or physical growth. But **without spiritual growth, we have no purpose in life.**

We will not all become Rockefellers or Bill Gates. We will not all become Arnold Schwarzeneggers or Charles Atlas. But we can **all** improve our spirituality and develop peace and contentment and happiness in our lives, even Bill Gates and Arnold. And isn't this what we all seek? Isn't the purpose of life to learn how to find **inner peace and contentment?**

When my brother who was alcoholic was dying, he finally found the inner peace and contentment that he had sought all his life. While on his deathbed, he pulled out his address book, picked up the telephone in the hospital and in the calmest manner; he tried to make calls to all his friends and family to tell them that he was departing this earthly life and wished to say goodbye to them and to thank them. To me, that required a tremendous amount of courage.

When I was finally able to get through to him on the phone, he told me quite calmly that the reason that his line was busy was because he had so many people to call. While I was in tears, he was calmly reassuring me not to worry and that everything would be all right. My brother who had sought meaningful change all his life, had finally found the true meaning of life on his deathbed. It is never too late to change!

In a previous chapter, I used the analogy of the old fisherman and the tourist to illustrate the point of material happiness versus spiritual happiness. In that story, the tourist was clearly materially better off than the old fisherman. But I assure you that the old man had found spiritual happiness, which is what the tourist was seeking. Having acquired as much material wealth as he needed, the tourist was now seeking spiritual happiness through change.

I am not suggesting for one minute that we should not all strive to improve our financial station in life or to improve our material well being. This is part of what growth is all about. I have a love of beautiful things as much as any other person. Of course the majority of us seek wealth and improvements in our financial and material well-being. **This after all is the American way of life**. But *wealth and material objects are only useful when we can share it with others and for the benefit of others.*

I recently visited a friend's open house. He had built a new house and I was aware of it but I had never actually seen the house; although I had been told that it was a very nice house. It turned out that he had invited a large number of his friends to the open house. **We were all impressed with the beauty of the house and stated as much.** *"How sad", I thought, "would it have been, if he had not been able to share the beauty of his house with others!"*

125

I am positive that he received greater satisfaction from having others appreciate and tell him what a beautiful house he had, than if he and his family were the only ones seeing the beauty therein. *The bible states that you should not hide your light under a bushel.*

Every one of us has the potential to achieve greatness in our lives. I stated in another chapter of this book that we can become as great as we dream. But we can only do this if we set our goals early, focus on our goals, plan for reaching our goals and follow the plan with minimal deviation from the map we create.

I had a patient of mine recently who had lost his job in the layoffs that followed September 11th. He was uncertain about what he wanted to do in the future and was in no hurry to seek a new job since he was financially well off.

When I asked him what he really wanted to do with the rest of his life, he replied, " If you must know, I would like to join the senior PGA tour for the over fifties players." "How wonderful!" I thought to myself, since this was also one of my fantasies **(duffer that I am, arthritis and all.)**

Now I know that I have stated that we can only be as great as we dream. But **since he was already past fifty** we both realized that entering the senior PGA tour for the over fifties was an unrealistic dream. **His ship had come and gone and there was only a canoe without a paddle waiting for him.** Nevertheless, not wishing to disprove my theory that we can all become as great as we dream **(and not wishing to discourage him)**, I encouraged him to go out there and practice everyday.

Hopefully when he becomes sixty, he could then enter the over sixties PGA tour!

When I conduct the mirror experiment with people, I ask them to visualize what they would like to be and how they would like to be **at a specific point in time in the future.** When I asked my fifty year old senior PGA tour hopeful to look in the mirror, it became immediately clear to him that his time had passed.

The only thing that he could look forward to was joining the **sixty-year-old** PGA tour players **in ten years time**. He finally settled on seeking a job as a golf equipment salesman. Since he already had previous experience in sales, had a wonderful personality and had some decent knowledge of golf equipment, I gave him my blessing and convinced him to go out and become the greatest golf equipment salesman ever.

He had at least ten years to practice his golf and he would have access to some of the best golf equipment to practice! Lucky him! Poor me!

The point I wish to make is that if we wish to achieve our goals, we need to define our goals early and set out on the path towards our goal early and to stay focused on our goal.

Personal satisfaction also comes from the feeling we get when we achieve our goals

through our own efforts. That is why handouts serve no useful purpose. I discuss this in the chapter titled, 'Give a man a fish versus teaching him to fish.' Our greatest satisfaction comes from the feeling we get when we have been responsible for creating our own destiny and achievements.

I love to paint and I have painted what my children have described as some of the ugliest paintings ever. I tell them that so did Picasso and Monet. But to me, my personal creations are greater than anything that Rembrandt or Picasso ever created. On the other hand, other people have been suitably impressed with my paintings and that also pleases me, when my work brings joy to others. Remember that Picasso was not appreciated until after his death. **I recommend anyone wishing a copy of my artwork to purchase it now, before I become more famous than Rembrandt (two thousand years from now).**

Careers

What happens when people achieve their goals? Should they sit back at this point, kick up their feet and relax in the contentment of their achievement? Or should they continue to grow through seeking meaningful achievements? Unless they do they are likely to suffer the same fate as those celebrities whose lives and careers went into a serious tailspin. This is what climbing mountains is all about. There are so many young multi-millionaires, from music, sports and the Internet boom period. These young people have acquired so much and so quickly, that if they do not seek to bring meaningful change into their lives, continually, they will find the disappointment of their decline so severe that they will rue the day they ever heard of Armani or Gucci.

Garth Brooks, one of the most prolific songwriters and the leading country music recording artist of all time sought to remake himself by changing his name to Chris Gaines and started producing rock music. He was a huge flop as Chris Gaines and reverted to his original name and his original style of music. *What was Garth trying to achieve when he changed his name and music? Garth was clearly seeking change.* As it turned out, what he did however was not meaningful change. Certain other events occurred in Garth Brooks' personal life at the same time, suggesting his desperate quest for change. *Hopefully this book will help Garth to understand the events that have occurred in his life and he will recognize what meaningful change is all about and will continue to entertain us with his fantastic talent.*

So many people achieve one goal in life and become placid and unmotivated to go on. The result of this attitude is what is commonly referred to as **'burnout.'** Looking at the graphic in Figure 1 and Figure 2, you can find where **you** are on the evolutionary path of change. If you find yourself at any point beyond the peak of the curve, then I suggest that it is time for you to conduct some serious introspection and seek some type of change in your life. Otherwise you may find yourself the subject of a story such as follows:

Two guys were sitting at a bar discussing the eulogy that was read at one of their friend's funeral. The first guy says to the other, " Do you know what I would like you to say at my eulogy?" "No, I don't," replied his friend. "What would you like me to say?"

"I would like you to say," said the first guy, "that I was a nice man, smart, kind, generous to a fault and a good family man."

"That's nice," said the second guy, "but do you know what I would like for you to say at my funeral?'

"What would you like for me to say?" asked the first guy.

" Well," says second guy, " I would like for you to say, Dang! I thought I saw him move!"

When I decided to give up a successful career in General Surgery because I felt that I had reached the top of my mountain and wanted to climb other mountains, my friends and family wondered whether I was going through mid-life crisis. **I guess that I must have as many lives as a cat, because my life has been one of repeated changes. This would be considered my third or fourth mid-life crisis**. But I am happy with my present station in life and I have glorious visions of my future.

When I look at some of my colleagues however and see the unhappiness in their outlook on life as far as their careers, **I can only wish that this book would help to put some direction into their lives. Do not be afraid to change!** But make sure that whatever change you make is **meaningful**. This does not mean that you have to completely change your career. But if you have to do so, my question to you is, **"So what?"**

Personal Relationships

If you wish to preserve the relationship that you are currently in or wish for your current relationship to grow, then you had better recognize the need for change. There is no place for complacency in relationships.

It is nothing short of remarkable to see people in relationships, where they profess great love for each other. Yet their relationship is dead, literally. I remember two couples that I admired for the outwards demonstration of love and devotion that I saw through their affection for each other and I remember feeling envy towards them. They seemed so in love with each other. They just could not be separated from each other. *They were always stuck together, like bread and butter. "Here were," I thought, "two perfect couples. How could they ever not be happy with each other?"*

Yet, a few years later, one couple was communicating with each other through written notes only, **which were stuck on the refrigerator**. The other couple, when I last saw them at a restaurant, would not look at each other. **They each conducted separate** conversations with me, oblivious to the presence of each other and frankly, I felt, each one wished that the other partner were dead.

"How tragic", I thought, "that such beautiful relationships are destroyed because individuals simply do not see the need for meaningful change and if they did, they know nothing about how to effect meaningful change."

What was most disturbing was that in each case, these were successful profession-als with successful second businesses. They understood how to run successful businesses but knew nothing about conducting successful personal relationships.

I have stated in other sections of this book, that the principles and process of change are the same, whether we apply them to individuals, their personal relationships, their careers, their businesses, their organizations or to society.

Sometimes we can't see the forest for the trees.

Businesses and Organizations

After I had started writing this book, I came across a book by Richard Tedlow, a historian and Professor of Business Administration at Harvard University. The title of the book is 'Giants of Enterprises.' This book is about seven business innovators and the empires they built. As Professor Tedlow stated in his book, the common thread that united these seven innovators, was their **willingness to embrace change**.

The seven giants were **Andrew Carnegie** (Carnegie foundation), **Sam Walton** (Wal-Mart), **Thomas J Watson Sr.** (IBM), **Charles Revson** (Revlon), **George Eastman** (Eastman-Kodak), **Robert Noyce** (Intel) and **Henry Ford** (Ford Motor Company).

"Henry Ford?" I thought. Here was a person who was considered as a giant of enterprise and had developed one of the most successful business enterprises. **Yet, the Detroit Lions football team, which was owned by the Ford family, is at the time of writing, the worst football team in the NFL with a 1-15 record.** Surely there must be a terrible disconnect here!

How is it that a family that develops one of the most successful business enterprises is unable to visualize the type of changes that would produce a successful football team?

And then the answer hit me flush between the eyes! Even successful businessmen fail to see that the principles and process of change that apply in the running of a successful business are the same principles and process <u>for every aspect of life</u>, including running sports teams.

As I reflect on the lives of these hugely successful businessmen, I wonder what was the quality of their personal relationships at home and whether any of them were divorced. **The answer to this question would tell me if they were really cognizant of the philosophy of meaningful change**. When I look at some other hugely successful individuals in our society, who forsook their previously good marriages in search of other partners, I know that these individuals do not know what meaningful change is all about. Neither do their partners.

Let us take a look at some other companies, both successes and failures or possible failures and examine the cause for their success or failure or decline.

In the motor vehicle industry for example, the big three have been Ford, Chrysler and GM. For years these companies were among the most successful in American industry. But either through a lack of perception of the need for change of their mental model or because of an unwillingness to change, they suddenly found themselves challenged by the Japanese car manufacturers and German car manufacturers.

Suddenly the Japanese and German car manufacturers who were producing smaller and more gasoline efficient vehicles besieged them. The mental model of the American car manufacturers told them that Americans wanted the big gas-guzzlers. It was not until these companies recognized the need for change that they were able to continue their growth.

And unless they recognize the need for continued meaningful change, they will eventually find themselves in a state of decline again.

Looking at the retail industry we see that in the not too distant past, the giants in this field were Sears and Roebuck, J.C Penney and K-Mart. For years these companies operated within a closed mental model that dictated how they conducted the bulk of their business. They understood how the major portion of their revenue was generated and saw no need to change with the changing times.

The result of this failure to change their mental model is that they are now playing catch-up with the likes of Wal-Mart, Cosco, Nordstrom and some online companies, which eroded their market share.

Before McDonald's restaurant became a household name throughout the world, the leader in the hamburger business was White Castle. **Outside of Ohio, I wonder how many people would even recognize the name 'White Castle?'**

Complacency results from **unwillingness to change** or **the inability to recognize the need to change**. White Castle's failure to operate within an open mental model led to the effective demise of this entity.

In order for Mc Donald's to continue its growth, it has introduced other items other than hamburgers into its menu. Whether or not they recognize this as a need to operate within an open mental model or whether they are acting instinctively, they are making necessary changes to continue to grow. Meaningful change will occur if the company understands the concept of the open versus closed mental model.

The technique that I use to help others see the need to change and to understand the process of change are the same graph of the product cycle that businesses use along with my 'magical' mirror experiment. *I utilize the tools that are utilized in negotiation and conflict resolution to encourage change in those who resist change. I utilize the tools from marketing to sell the idea of change to those who need to see the benefits of change.*

I no longer try to force people to change. I no longer **tell** people to change. I **show** them why they need to change and I help them **to see how** to change. I try to get people to make a **voluntary** decision to change. **This is called empowerment**. As I have stated repeatedly in this book, **force does not produce meaningful change**. Getting people to change their mental models is what results in meaningful change.

The reason that we as physicians have **failed** miserably to cure depression and to achieve better success rates in smoking cessation is because while **we are great at telling** people what to do and what not to do, we are **horrible at showing** people why they should choose alternative behaviors. And **we are even worse at showing them how to** effect meaningful change.

Human nature dictates that few individuals embrace change willingly. As I point out in earlier sections of this book, change carries with it a certain element of risk. Many people prefer the status quo! **Getting people to accept the need for change therefore requires "buy-in"**.

In order to get others to embrace change, we have to get them to buy-in to the ideas that we are selling them. There are various marketing skills that we can use to get people to buy-in. These are basic marketing and negotiation skills. The more knowledgeable we are in our understanding of negotiation and marketing principles, the more likely are we to succeed in getting others to accept the need for change.

As an example of how I utilize these techniques in my practice, consider the following case: *'A young female patient entered my office and immediately demanded "I want something for my stress!" I enquired as to the cause of her problem and she bluntly re-iterated, " I am under a lot of stress and I want something for my stress!" She proceeded to enumerate all the various stressors in her life.*

I responded that the medication that she wanted was not going to provide a meaningful solution to her problem, to which she retorted, "So you mean to tell me that you are not going to give me anything for my problem?"

I reassured her that I was going to address her problem but that what I was going to give her would be more meaningful in providing a solution to her present problems and how she dealt with problems in future.

At this point she broke into tears because she was convinced that I was not going to *give her what she <u>wanted</u>, which was pills. I on the other hand was determined to give her what she <u>needed</u>.*

I pleaded with her to give me a chance to show her that I was receptive to her problems and begged her to listen to what I was trying to tell her. Having convinced her that I was not ignoring her problems but that I was genuinely concerned with helping her find solutions to her problems, she calmed down and listened to what I had to say.

I then proceeded to go through step by step the process of change until I could show her that significant and meaningful change was possible and that she had the power to implement the changes that were necessary for her to have a less stressful and more enjoyable life. The end result was dramatic!

This originally angry woman who stormed into my office, left my office smiling and full of hope for the future. She left with more than what she came to my office for and I was able to give her exactly what she needed. She was extremely grateful and I was gratified with the results'.

I must explain part of the reason for this patient's attitude stemmed from the fact that she had been seen by other doctors who had become increasingly frustrated by what they perceived as her demanding behavior.

As a result, these doctors had become increasingly reluctant to give her the pills that she was demanding. **The problem is that they did not understand how to give the patient what she really needed and consequently she was given nothing at all**. This is how she ended up in my office as my patient. I am only too happy to accept these "non-compliant" and manipulative patients, as they are described in our profession, into my practice.

Why is it so difficult to get others to understand the need for meaningful change and why are even successful business people unable to make meaningful change in areas outside of their business?

The answer lies in the lack of **properly trained** guides. I describe my role to my patients as that of a guide rather than a doctor. **I also describe myself as a gas station owner** who operates the gas station where they come for a fill-up when their tanks are running low on their long journey. This both amuses and relaxes them.

Before I settled in the United States of America, I had lived in Guyana, Jamaica, Barbados, Scotland, England and I had spent considerable time in Trinidad and Tobago and Canada. **(Talk about change.)**

The people in the countryside of Barbados, bless their hearts are some of the sweetest, kindest, most helpful people in the world. They remind me of so many of my colleagues in the medical profession.

132

The people from the countryside of Barbados are so helpful that if you asked them for directions they would never tell you they did not know, *even when they had no idea where you wanted to go, just like so many of my colleagues in the medical profession.* They were always willing to help, just like my colleagues in the medical profession.

Here is an example of how a Barbadian from the countryside would give directions to someone if he/she were asked *(and sometimes even when they are not asked):*

Tourist: *"Excuse me sir! Could you direct me to Mr. Jonathan Smith's home?"*

Barbadian bystander (who doesn't have a clue where you wish to go): *"Mr. Smith's home? No problem man. Listen well. You go about four to five miles down the road. When you come to the first left turn, don't take that one. That's not it. You will come to another left turn. It isn't that one either. Go another nine to ten minutes until you come to a brown house with a little boy flying a kite there. It isn't there. Travel a little ways further until you come to a right hand turn. Don't take that one. Take the next right turn and go about five, maybe ten minutes until you come upon a windmill. You will see a white cow grazing in a field there.* When you get there, ask anyone for directions. Anyone will be able to tell you how to get to Mr. Smith's house."

I regret to say that this is the type of direction that people have been getting when they seek advice on how to effect meaningful change. The Barbadian country folk genuinely wish to be helpful. **Doctors and psychologists are no less guilty of giving poor advice than some of the consultants who have been paid large sums of money for advice to organizations that are failing. Unlike some of the consultants who accept large sums of money for work that they <u>know</u> is useless, most physicians genuinely wish to help patients.**

But like the Barbadian country folk offering advice, they need to understand how to give directions before trying to do so. In fairness to Barbadian country folk, I must say that this is the same attitude of country folk everywhere and as I have stated, I have lived in many parts of the world and I love country folk. They really do understand the true meaning of life.

Before we can teach others how to make meaningful change in their lives, we need to understand how to make meaningful change **in our own lives**. Before we can give people directions on how to get to a particular destination, we our selves must know how to get there. **I will not pretend to have been any different until I saw the need for change in my self.**

The blind cannot lead the blind. Worse yet, the dead cannot lead the blind!

Society

As far as the need for change in our society, I can only state that **if it is not obvious by now that major changes of a meaningful type are needed in our society, then I am preaching to the choir. September 11th should serve as a stimulus for us all to seek meaningful change in our society.**

September 11th provided us with an **opportunity** to see how we could be truly united as a society. In our time of crisis, we all held out a helping hand to each other. **We wore symbolic U.S flag pins proudly on our chests and sang "God Bless America lustily."**

Sad to say, three months had not passed before the lawyers were drawing up their briefs **(not the ones they wear)** and preparing to sue anyone who could spell Twin Towers. *Crisis made us learn to be connected but crisis does not lead to meaningful change. Teaching people why and how to change does.*

I can only pray that our nation and the world will recognize that for us to grow and develop, that we need to learn how to effect meaningful change.

Let's take another case of the teenage boy who was having a difficult relationship with his girlfriend and his father. He was depressed and stressed because he found out that his girlfriend had been seeing someone else. She had expressed remorse and had promised to be faithful in the future but he was doubtful whether he could totally accept the situation even though he professed his love for her. He was also having a difficult relationship with his father because he felt that his father was applying undue pressure in his life as far as trying to plan his future, college-wise and work-wise.

This situation is all too common and results in tremendous stress on individuals. He absolutely did not want to have any type of relationship with his father who he felt was completely fixed and set in his ways and would not even want to change.

I needed to convince this individual that because his life was so miserable that he absolutely needed to change his mental model if he was going to be happy. I also had to convince him that his girlfriend and father needed to change and that it was possible for him to help them see the need for them to do so.

I showed him that if everyone could make the necessary commitment to make meaningful change that they would all benefit. I walked him through the process of change and eventually led him to the "mirror experiment". I eventually showed him that if everyone concerned was prepared to make meaningful change, that it would result in a win-win situation for all concerned.

It took me all of one hour, working through my lunchtime to get that young man to be willing to change his fixed assumptions regarding his father and girlfriend.

When I finally got him to the point of expressing his willingness or desire to change, I knew that I had an opportunity to effect meaningful change, not only in that young man but also in his girlfriend and father.

It was a very painstaking process taking that young man to the point where I felt I had made a significant change in his mental model. But it was worth every minute of my time and his time. **Suicide is a very common problem among our youth. This drastic action results when the individuals see no hope for meaningful changes in their lives. We owe it to each other to help each other to make meaningful changes in our lives.**

If we would make a genuine effort to understand the philosophy and process of change and if we sought to make meaningful change, starting with our self, we as individuals, our personal relationships, our careers, our businesses, our institutions, our organizations and our world, will be so much better for the change.

> **'And the world, will be a better place
> For you, for me, you just wait and see.'**

CHAPTER 13

Depression, Diabetes, Diseases and the Need for Change

The Emperor and his new Clothes.

And then the little boy whispered to his mother, "Mommy, mommy the emperor is naked." And the mother whispered back, "Hush child, someone might hear you!"
Grimm's Fairy Tales.

The existing paradigm in medicine today teaches us that depression is caused by a chemical imbalance in the brain. Hogwash I say! Oops, I am starting to think like Galileo and he was nearly killed for suggesting that the world was round. I suspect that there may be many psychiatrists out there who would like to do the same to me.

We have bought into this paradigm about depression and anxiety being caused by a chemical imbalance in the brain in the same way that others believed that AIDS was a curse from God. We have been told so often that depression and anxiety and every other behavioral disorder is caused by a chemical imbalance in the brain that we actually believe this is true.

We are also told that Alcoholism is genetic and that scientists have discovered the gene for alcoholism. **They have even discovered the gene for obesity! Sixty percent of Americans are overweight or obese. Is this gene unique to the USA? Why hasn't this gene manifested itself in Somalia and the Sudan? And how about India and China the two most heavily populated countries in the world?**

Maybe with the entrance of Mc Donald's and Burger King into these countries, we might see the transference of the obesity gene into those countries. Maybe the obesity gene is carried on cheeseburgers; or something in potato chips induces a change in our genetic structure just like how some of the new diabetes medicines alter some genes in our body.

Whatever happened to the good old-fashioned theory that obesity comes from drinking too much beer and eating too many potato chips and then lying about on the couch all day long watching Sunday afternoon football. Who really believes this garbage? I suppose that if we say it long enough and often enough it will all be true.

Or what about obesity being caused from going to the numerous buffet restau-

rants and figuring that you have just got to sample the one hundred items on the menu and just for good measure, you must have second helpings, simply because you paid your $7.50 and you simply have to get your money's worth.

I have patients coming into my practice with newspaper clippings and clippings from the National Enquirer, telling me that they have a chemical imbalance in their brain and this is why their relationships are failing. No one tells you anymore that they are having problems with meeting their credit card payments or that their husbands are having affairs or that 'Poochie' the family pet had to be put to sleep because he was too old. **It's that chemical imbalance thing!**

They request a pill to change the chemical imbalance that is causing them to eat too many chocolates and potato chips. They request a pill to control that child who comes home to an empty house and like any warm blooded child seeks out mischief to relieve his boredom. **Suddenly that child has ADHD.**

I have looked at numerous children who have been diagnosed with ADHD and the common thread that I have seen; **in the vast majority of cases** is the **lack of good parenting skills.** In our schools today, our teachers are prepared to ignore any meaningful attempts to get the so-called ADHD kids to learn why and how they need to make meaningful change and **prefer to use chemical restraints such as Ritalin on these kids**.

They would rather focus on the kids who are doing well and ignore the kids who really need help. After all, this requires much less effort, doesn't it? I say that we have got our world turned upside down. I say that we should focus more effort on the kids who really need help. The other kids are better prepared to take care of themselves. **It doesn't only make good economic sense; it is the right thing to do!**

Isn't this the same thing in our criminal justice system where criminals are locked up in jails and are released back into society after serving brief periods of their sentences, without any meaningful change in their behavior, simply because the jails are too overcrowded?

In my practice today, I focus on taking the **worst patients and making them the best**. I will refuse **no one** entrance into my practice. To me this makes good economic sense, because in a managed care setting, **if I decrease my pool of bad patients by making them better, then I automatically increase my pool of good patients, without having to go out and seek new patients.**

This makes good business sense and is also absolutely the right thing to do. Yet **so many physicians prefer not to treat Medicaid patients** but will still complain when their income continues to shrink because managed care continues to reduce their reimbursement per patient.

Instead, they scramble over each other like crabs in a barrel, trying to get an increased share of the limited pool of 'good' patients in an increasingly competitive market.

In the medical community today, our first inclination is to prescribe pills for every disease under the sun, when pills should be the last resort. I don't claim to have been any different from my colleagues in the way I practiced medicine previously. **But I have changed** and I believe that **we all can change** and I believe that we all **should** change.

Why would I not be surprised if a gene was soon discovered that is responsible for companies going bankrupt? Or we may discover that it was bacteria that caused American Airlines to develop financial problems after September 11th. **But then again, that is not really far from the truth, when we consider the anthrax scare that followed in the aftermath of September 11th!**

Am I the only person who can see that the emperor has no clothes? I would like to use a stronger term for how I think about these theories but **I resolved to keep this book clean!**

I come from a family of ten children and only **one** became an alcoholic! Is my father or mother supposed to feel guilty that they passed on this gene to only one child out of ten?

I can name so many large families that I deal with where only one member demonstrated addictive tendencies and yet we are expected to believe these theories from the so called experts. "Baloney!" I say. Let the "experts" eat cake! **Who are these experts anyway? I prefer the definition of an expert as, "someone who know more and more about less and less."**

Do we still want to believe that the world is flat? Wake up people! If we believe these hogwash theories, then it is no wonder that the recurrence rates and the failure rates for these diseases are so high. The stated recurrence rate if you have one episode of major depression is 50%. **Wow!** The psychiatrists are proud to recite these figures repeatedly. **It sets up the depressed and anxious patient for failure immediately.**

It is not the patient who has failed; it is the psychiatrist and whoever else treats depression and anxiety that has failed! It is the cardiologist who has failed when the patient returns repeatedly for a failed stent procedure.

It is time that we own up to the fact that it is our own shortcomings in our lack of understanding of how to effect meaningful change in these patients, that is responsible for the high failure rate and the high recurrence rates!

I dare to be different and challenge all these so-called expert theories! Like Galileo I am not afraid to stand alone!

The Pharmaceutical companies are only too happy to pay for studies to support such wild claims because this helps to keep patients on their high priced drugs forever. After all, stock prices have to be maintained for the investors! Meantime, not only do the patients receive inadequate care, but also the whole economy suffers.

We are told that the depressed patient must be kept on these expensive medications for at least six to nine months to achieve success and even in spite of this the failure rate is still a full 50%. And the recurrence rate if you have more than two episodes of depression is close to one hundred percent. Amazing! **We are so proud of the ineffectiveness of our methods of treating depression and the ineffectiveness of the high priced medicines that we boast about our failure rates.**

If you took your car to the mechanic for repairs and after the third episode he told you that the chance of your car breaking down on the highway is one hundred percent or even fifty percent, would you be happy. I think not!

What this all means is that once a patient is diagnosed with one of these psychological disorders, the pharmaceutical companies are guaranteed a customer for at least nine months and **potentially for life.**

It is no wonder that so called "specialists" are afforded such generous handouts to come up with their exotic and ludicrous theories regarding so many disease states. **The paid vacations offered to physicians to come up with these ludicrous theories are just as exotic as the theories themselves.**

I begin to wonder which company sponsored the studies that suggest that bacteria are responsible for causing heart disease. **Could it possibly be a pharmaceutical company that manufactures drugs for treating infectious diseases?**

To suggest that the chemical imbalance in the brain is the cause of depression is akin to saying that a high blood sugar is the cause of diabetes. It does not require a great deal of thought or common sense to recognize that a high blood sugar is not the cause of diabetes but that it is the **result** of diabetes. **Even Tattoo on Fantasy Island could figure that one out!**

Why is it then that so many prominent psychiatrists and scientists teach us that depression is caused by a chemical imbalance in the brain? Which came first, the chicken or the egg?

I know that I am likely to raise the ire of my very eminent colleagues in the field of psychiatry and cardiology when I suggest that we should debunk the theories that depression is caused by a chemical imbalance of the brain or that bacteria cause coronary artery disease, but I will think like the futurist that I am and project that like so many of our past assumptions in medicine, that this is another that will be ultimately proven to be wrong and eventually buried in the graveyard of "Medical Myths." I say once again. "The emperor has no clothes!"

If I am proved correct in the future, I will likely to be pronounced a prophet long after I am dead and gone, just like Van Gogh was recognized as a great artist only after he was long dead and gone.

139

I hope to convince my eminent colleagues that what I am suggesting here needs closer scrutiny and until we recognize that we have been wrong in so many of our past assumptions, then we will not be able to implement the correct treatment that will make meaningful change in our patients' lives.

Until we implement the true corrective treatment for our patients' illnesses, such as depression and anxiety, heart disease and obesity, and ADHD and gastro-esophageal reflux disease (simple heartburn), then we will continue to see the high recurrence rates and treatment failures that accompany these diseases.

And the cost of medical care will escalate to such a point that a crisis similar to September 11th will develop in the medical profession and we all know what is the result of crisis.

At this point I am no longer talking philosophy. I stopped talking philosophy since Chapter 1. What I am talking here is economics and finance! I am talking common sense! We are hurting our pockets and we don't even know it.

Just in case you may have forgotten, **crisis forces change** and more often than not, the change that results from crisis is shocking and unpleasant.

We need a paradigm shift. In keeping with my original postulate that all assumptions will eventually be proved false, I suggest that **the chemical imbalance in the brain is not the cause** of depression but the effect of depression **and is merely a symptom of the disease.**

When we use chemicals to alter the chemical imbalance in the brain, we are simply treating the symptoms of a disease for which we truthfully have never understood its true etiology.

I know that I am likely to be accused of blasphemy but **I am willing to adopt the same position as Galileo who once dared to make the ludicrous comment that the world was round and not flat!** Who ever heard of such a ludicrous statement?

I am reminded of how we were once taught that Type 2 diabetes was caused by a deficiency of insulin. The new teaching is that Type 2 diabetics initially, actually have higher insulin levels in their blood and that insulin resistance rather than lack of insulin is the cause of their diabetes, as we were once taught.

I can only speculate what **future** scientists will teach us about the etiology and treatment of diabetes. Maybe they will soon discover that bacteria cause diabetes as soon as some pharmaceutical company funds such a study and can find someone to produce such results. Remember when we were taught that peptic ulcers were the result of increased acidity in the stomach?

Today we are told that peptic ulcers are caused from bacteria. And now we are told that coronary artery disease might be caused from bacteria. **What next?**

Could an infective agent also cause obesity and depression? Does this question really sound as ludicrous as it should or could it possibly be true that if we persist with our current trend of discoveries as to the causes of disease that this might be future teaching to medical students and physicians?

If I suggest that depression is not caused by a chemical imbalance in the brain and if I suggest that a chemical imbalance is not responsible for causing anxiety and social phobias, then what do I suggest is the cause?

I suggest that **depression, anxiety, social phobias, claustrophobia and a host of other psychiatric disorders are caused by a feeling of hopelessness that results from the feeling of a loss of control of one's life and a failure to see workable solutions, that is, failure to see the possibility of meaningful change. The same situation exists when personal relationships fail or companies go bankrupt.**

When I explained to some of my colleagues and some patients and friends of the need for a paradigm shift, I was asked if I was now advocating and practicing alternative medicine. The answer is a blunt no! **I am not advocating alternative medicine.**

I am advocating an alternative approach to how we view and treat diseases. We need to get out of our nineteenth century mentality and emerge into the twenty-first century.

My observation of depression, anxiety, phobias, stress, inability to cope and a multitude of other mental disorders is that they all result from loss of the feeling of control and the inability to see the opportunity for effecting meaningful change in individuals' lives. **This loss of control and the inability to effect meaningful change lies at the root of these common disorders.**

The classic example of how loss of control and inability to effect meaningful change results in anxiety, is seen in airplane passengers. Why do airline passengers experience so much anxiety? The answer lies in their perception that when they are in a plane, they have absolutely no control and should anything happen to the pilot or the plane; they would have no opportunity to make any meaningful difference.

Who likes the idea of sitting in a metal box, thirty six thousand feet up in the air with a guy in charge who possibly had a fight with his wife earlier in the day and who is responsible for taking us to our destination? I don't. Do you?

Do we feel the same when we are driving a motorcar? Certainly not! At least most of us who drive motorcars have less anxiety when we are behind the wheel of our car than when we are in planes.

Why else, after September 11th did most people prefer to drive than to fly? *What happened to suddenly cause the sudden shift in the chemical balance in all of these*

141

people's brain?

If depression, anxiety, phobias and other psychiatric disorders are not caused by a chemical imbalance in the brain and if we recognize that the symptoms that these people experience are the result of their feelings of hopelessness and inability to effect meaningful change in their lives; what does this say about how we have been treating these patients for years?

Well! Guess what? We have been feeding our patients some very potent and potentially noxious medicines for years and these trusting patients have faithfully taken these potentially harmful medicines because as they have told us repeatedly, **"You should know best doctor. You are the doctor and I trust you!"**

Well doctor, we have been wrong repeatedly over the years. And unless we make that paradigm shift that I mentioned earlier we will continue to be wrong! **And we will continue to tighten the noose around our collective necks in the medical profession and the only people we should blame should be us.**

Isn't it a strange paradox that in our school system where we constantly teach children to say no to drugs, that teachers are insisting that students take **mind-altering** drugs. **I am talking about Ritalin and Adderal and every other type of stimulant drug;** which have become the drugs of choice in our school system today.

Kids are selling Ritalin to each other in our schools today. **What happened in our society to suddenly cause this epidemic of ADHD in our schools today compared to the past?** And why is this disease not as prevalent in the lesser-developed countries? **Under-diagnosis you say?**

Could it possibly be that these countries; which cannot afford the expensive medications have developed more effective techniques for implementing meaningful change in their youngsters, techniques that we have forgotten and have abandoned in the name of civil liberties? **We live in the freest country of the world but I have always maintained that freedom without boundaries equals chaos.** Have you ever tried to play a game of football in which there are no rules and there are no boundaries to the field. That is how we are playing our games in trying to teach our children today.

Our educational system needs serious overhaul. Our teachers need to understand the concept of meaningful change and need to be taught how to show kids **why** and **how** they should seek to effect meaningful change. **They need to understand that when kids fail, it is a reflection of the failure of the teacher and the parent, not the child.**

Teachers, accept responsibility for learning how to effect meaningful change and you will help to create a better society for all of us! I make the same statement to parents. *And I say the same thing to physicians who bow to the teachers demand that we should impose chemical restraints on our children.* I am willing to introduce any teacher who wishes to learn how to effect meaningful change, *in the worst children,* to a program called 'Boysville of Michigan' where the caregivers take the worst kids in society and make them into examples to be proud of.

I am by no means encouraging the methods employed in Singapore but I suggest to you that you are unlikely to find people littering the streets of Singapore. And chewing gum on the streets of Singapore is certainly not a major problem.

Frankly I am more afraid of the ADHD bacteria infecting our schoolchildren than I am afraid of smallpox or anthrax!

Godzilla and little Charlie.

'I was asked to see a six-year-old boy who his teachers wanted to be placed on Ritalin. Charlie's mother brought him to me but she was reluctant to have her child put on Ritalin. The teachers however insisted that if Charlie was not put on the drug, that he would be kicked out of school.

Initially, little Charlie's mom decided to accompany him to school and sat with him in class. She told me that when she sat in the class with her son, there was no problem with his work or his behavior. As she stated, she was able to keep him focused on his tasks. She stated that little Charlie's problem in school was that very often he didn't find the work that the class was doing to be very interesting and he would amuse himself with other activities. I asked her to bring the young tyke to my office so that I could observe his abnormal behavior.

While little Charlie was in my office, I observed him walking with his arms outstretched in front of him, lifting one leg at a time and planting it firmly on the ground before lifting and planting the other one. While he was doing this, he kept making loud 'whooshing' noises. "Whoosh, whoosh, whoosh," went little Charlie, constantly, while his mom and I discussed his problems. This went on for a while until I asked Charlie what he was doing. Charlie answered that he was acting the role of Godzilla, his favorite TV character. He also stated that he loved dinosaurs and loved to read about dinosaurs. He said that he loved everything about dinosaurs.

His mom confirmed that Charlie did in fact love dinosaurs and this was the only thing that could capture his attention absolutely. When I asked the mother why the school did not use dinosaurs to teach Charlie to read and count, she replied that the teachers had in fact taken all the books on dinosaurs out of the classroom. *Apparently the teachers had decided that little Charlie had "an obsessive compulsive disorder about dinosaurs." "Since when," I asked his mother, " was it abnormal for a little six year old boy, to act out his childhood fantasies?"*

I asked Charlie's mom if the behavior that the child was displaying in my office was the type of behavior that the school psychologist and teachers considered abnormal and she replied positively.'

I asked her to set up appointments for the teachers to come to my office so that I could treat the teachers instead of Charlie! The alternative was for me to introduce them to 'Boysville of Michigan.'

If the answer is to increase the number of teachers in the school system and to have them properly trained, I suggest that we should do it! The amount of money our states would save through the <u>decreased</u> use of Ritalin and other drugs of this type and the economic and social benefit to society, would more than justify the cost.

Fearful Freddie

And why do husbands who try to teach their wives to drive make absolutely the worst driving instructors and navigators for their wives? Isn't it because of the anxiety that they feel because they have given up control of the vehicle to their wives?

As a result they are reduced to a quivering, anxious mass of Jell-O, screaming epithets at their wives because they are anticipating an accident at any moment; and because the wife is the boss, she completely ignores the husband and they (the husbands) can do absolutely nothing, meaningful or otherwise to change the situation.

Even if they were allowed to make a suggestion, the wife would not listen anyway!

So how do we treat our depressed, anxious, stressed out patients? Of course; **give them a pill!** This is the quick, easy answer. Have we changed anything? **Certainly! We changed the chemical imbalance in their brain!** But did we make a meaningful change in our patients? Absolutely not! They still remain with their miserable lives **but they feel better about it.**

Soon, the medicines no longer work for them and so they return for us to increase the dose or change to another pill or add another pill to their increasing collection of pills. They feel better for a while until sexual dysfunction sets in and begins to affect their personal relationships further. Often they gain enormous amounts of weight.

This then aggravates their depression and so they return to us for more pills to treat their increased chemical imbalance in their brain. In a fee for service environment, this is good business for us. But in the managed care setting, these patients are a disaster for us. **So in return, we too become depressed and vow that we are going to quit medicine forever.**

One of my patients, Roger (a pseudonym), who I will mention in more detail later, told me that when he sought help from counselors for his addiction to narcotic drugs and alcohol, their solution was to prescribe him **LIBRIUM!**

As he so eloquently put it, **"Doc, when I was battling my addiction, they were feeding me with drugs that promote addiction!"**

Roger was perceptive enough and lucky enough that he was able to break the cycle of addiction, **no thanks to his counselors and physicians.**

The cost for treating depressive illnesses is currently approximately $42 billion. This constitutes a significant portion of the health care budget. This is only the direct cost of treating depression. The economic cost from the social fallout of poorly treated depression is incalculable. Even Alan Greenspan couldn't figure that one out. This is money that indirectly comes out of our pockets. Add the cost of treating heartburn, a disease (?) which can be treated in the vast majority of cases simply by controlling how much pizza and beer you consume, with some of the most expensive drugs and we are talking big bucks here. (And I am not talking about deer hunting!)

Do you know what? That money is coming out of all of our pockets, physicians, patients, lawyers and politicians and even the pharmaceutical representatives and pharmaceutical companies

Are there alternatives to the self-destructive behavior that we are currently indulging in? If I didn't think that this is so, I would not have stayed up many long hours at night wasting my time writing this book, when I could have enjoyed some good nights sleep rather than waking up bleary-eyed in the morning trying to go to work on time.

We fail to see the benefits of trying to effect meaningful change in our patients but we scream at the HMOs and the Government because they are seeking to reduce Healthcare costs. If we can see and understand the doctrine of change and the process of change, we have the opportunity to help our patients to effect meaningful change in their disease states and we can save ourselves a whole lot of money in the process.

Remember, when I said earlier that I stopped talking philosophy and I am now talking pure economics. Doesn't it make economic sense that we need to seek meaningful change?

We can only effect meaningful change in others when we are prepared to change ourselves first. We need to change our mental model!

While writing this book, I had a very enlightening discussion with the patient Roger, who I mentioned earlier. This was a most fascinating individual. I will call him Roger although he has stated that I could portray him as what meaningful change is all about and he gave me permission to use his real name.

This gentleman is one of the best patients I have ever had to deal with. He is compliant in every aspect of his care and I have had some of the most enlightening discussions with him. Whenever he shows up at my office for his appointments, I cannot help but spend a few extra minutes in casual conversation with him.

This of course makes my staff madder than Osama running around in a cold Afghan cave, because I invariably end up running behind time. But Roger is such a fascinating person that I feel that at every encounter with him, I end up learning as much from him as he learns from me.

Roger was a former dope addict who had been clean for over ten years. He had spent thirteen years of his life in and out of jail. He quit drugs, alcohol and tobacco and decided to pursue a healthy lifestyle.

He became a fitness fanatic and exercised regularly, got married, had children and became a counselor for other drug addicts and alcoholics. He never missed an appointment and whenever he showed up for his appointments, he was always immaculately dressed and well groomed.

When I discussed the principles of change and the process of change with this gentleman, I was amazed at the amount of insight that he possessed. He understood instinctively, all of the principles that I have outlined in this book and was applying these principles in his own life.

He never learned these principles formally but knew **instinctively** what he needed to do to make the changes in his life meaningful and long lasting.

What I found most fascinating was the fact that he recognized that the most meaningful change resulted from his recognition of his need to change his mental model, although this was not the term he used. He pointed to his head and said, **"Doc, this is what you have to change."** The other fact that I found remarkable was the comment he made, **"You know doc, I realized that you <u>can't stop</u> changing. You have to work at it every day to keep changing."**

I recognized that this former dope addict understood the principle and process of change better than many professionals and many of the psychologists and psychiatrists who were dealing with these types of patients.

I knew that my friend Roger was a lucky person and that his future was bright. I knew that **my role as his physician was merely to be his guide if he strayed** and I knew that with his insight that this was unlikely.

I thought how lucky he was and I felt saddened when I realized how many more Rogers are out there who only need to be shown the process of **how to make meaningful change** in their lives but were being deprived of the opportunity to do so **because the people who were supposed to be helping them did not themselves understand the process.**

Our prison system is full of other Rogers on whom our criminal justice system is seeking to force change. As I have stated before, **force and threats and coercion only result in short term change at the best. Meaningful change results when we can teach others why they need to change, show them the benefits of change help them to plan for change and help them to implement their plan and to recognize that meaningful change is an ongoing process.**

When I told Roger that I was amazed at **his** understanding of the principles and process of change, his reply was, **"Doc, I am surprised that YOU know so much about change!"** I smiled and thanked Roger for the lessons he had taught me.

Diabetes, hypertension, coronary artery disease, obesity, cigarette smoking and a host of other conditions all fall into the same category as depression.

As physicians, when we treat diabetes, heart disease, high blood pressure, high cholesterol, obesity, tobacco abuse heartburn and a host of other diseases, we should really be teaching our patients how to effect meaningful changes in their lives so that they could be empowered to take control of their diseases.

Instead, what do we do as physicians? We give the patients pills and we instruct them how to take these pills. We give them cursory instructions about diet and exercises. **We** tell **them** what **we** want them to do rather than **showing** them **why** and **how** to make the changes that would lead to real differences in their health care.

'When I was a little boy and my mother told me never to do something, it was then that I was most likely to do it; because I figured that if she didn't want me to do it, then there must be something good that she was trying to deprive me of pleasure.

When we tell our patients not to indulge in self-destructive behavior, they are no different from little children and they feel that we are trying to punish them and trying to deprive them of pleasure.

Consequently, they refuse to follow our instructions and we are forced to continue prescribing expensive medicines and the cardiologists keep bringing them back for their tenth cardiac catheterizations and their sixth angioplasty (rotor-router operation on their arteries).

When they fail to follow our instructions, we call them **"non-compliant"** and threaten to discharge them from our practices, especially if they belong to HMOs. In other words, **we try to force these patients to change**. I have stated repeatedly throughout this book that **forcing people to change does not result in meaningful change.**

How much better would it not be if we can **teach** others how to make meaningful change in their lives? **How much fewer noxious, costly and unnecessary medications would we not be able to discard if we can teach people the "Process of change"?**

How much more efficient would be our care if we could show people how and why they should seek to change? How much better would be the quality of our care?

How many billions in healthcare dollars would we be able to save if people learnt the benefits and the techniques of effecting meaningful change? And how much more money would we make when we practice better medicine?

Understanding the principles and process of meaningful change will result in more efficient, cost effective and better quality care in medicine. We have the capacity to save billions of dollars from doing this. **It doesn't only make economic sense. It is the right thing to do.**

We can use the money saved to provide access to health care to the millions who are currently without this and <u>we can do this without draining one cent more from the national budget.</u>

The cost savings can be transferred to our motor industry, which currently spends more money on health care than it does on steel.

And what about the Pharmaceutical Companies? Well, they can continue to make huge profits if they direct their research to provide effective medicines to treat other types of diseases, **rather than us having ten companies producing the same type of ulcer medicines or anti-depressants and other 'me too' drugs, simply because it is the easiest thing to do, rather than the right thing to do.**

And they can direct their attention to providing medicines at cheaper cost to treat the billions around the world who do not have access to even the most basic medicines. **Yes, it is our problem and we should care! That would be meaningful change.**

When Eli Lilly and company developed the pill called Zyprexa, that was meaningful change, because this drug is unique in its class and is very useful in treating psychotic patients. When Eli Lilly developed Prozac, that was also meaningful change, since the drugs that were previously used to treat depression, all had noxious side effects.

On the other hand *when Eli Lilly obtained FDA approval for a name change from Prozac to Sarafem when the Prozac patent was about to expire, I do not consider that to be meaningful change. Similarly, When ten other pharmaceutical companies develop pills with basically the same properties as Prozac, simply because the Anti-depressant market is so huge, that too is not meaningful change.*

But the most meaningful change in healthcare will come about when we as physicians and we as a society will accept the challenge of providing access to basic healthcare universally. We need to not only address the healthcare needs of the thirty-five to forty million Americans without medical insurance but also the millions around the world. **I stress that it is our problem. We can ignore the message at our**

own peril.

The fact remains that we can achieve these goals with minimal if any increase in our current spending. We simply need to refocus on how we currently treat many disease states and seek a more efficient system of providing care using some of the techniques I have suggested. The economic benefits can be huge and **no one needs to lose**.

Learning the "Process of Change" and spending a few extra minutes to teach people how to effect meaningful change can actually be a profitable business and would also give us a greater sense of personal satisfaction. We will grow economically but more importantly, we will grow spiritually because we would know that we are really making a real difference in the transformation of our world into a better place for us all. That would be meaningful change.

I challenge the Pharmaceutical Industry to step up and become real leaders in medical care. I challenge the medical profession to step forwards and become real leaders in healthcare. I challenge patients to empower themselves and accept direct responsibility for their health. I challenge myself to continue to seek to effect meaningful change in me and in others. I accept the challenge. Will you?

Figure 8

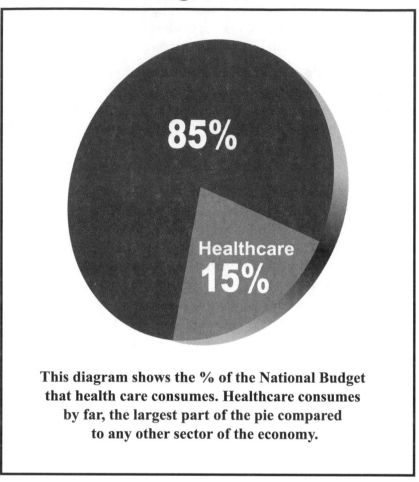

85%

Healthcare
15%

This diagram shows the % of the National Budget
that health care consumes. Healthcare consumes
by far, the largest part of the pie compared
to any other sector of the economy.

When compared to all other sectors of the economy, healthcare consumes the largest portion of the national pie. This sector continues to devour a greater portion of the pie and left unchecked will result in chaos. Healthcare at this point is heading to a crisis. The only way to halt and reverse the process is through meaningful change in the profession.

CHAPTER 14

Leadership and Change

During the time that I was in the process of writing this book, I came across an article in the Wall Street Journal in the section titled, "Work and Family". The title of the article was **"How to help kids with the right stuff grow into leaders."**

The author of the article, was commenting on what she perceived to be a problem and that was the fact that her thirteen-year-old daughter had expressed the desire to be president. **According to the mother and author, people kept dumping on her daughter's dream and as one adult had told her daughter, "you'll never raise enough money." A schoolmate had said, "You'll be assassinated because you are a woman."**

She, the author questioned whether in times (September 11th) that called for great leadership whether we as adults were preparing kids well as the political, civic and public-service leaders. She further commented that researchers and professionals had concluded from studies that children and teens were not getting as much practice at leadership in the past. 'Only 1.5% of today's young college graduates have ever worked on a political campaign, based on a study of 40,000 recent grads, by Robert Zemsky, a University of Pennsylvania professor and Peterson's, a learning-resource unit of Thompson Corp., Toronto.

The author lamented the fact that with today's huge high schools, there were fewer and fewer opportunities for children to assume leadership roles in the larger schools. "There can only be one class president of the senior class," and with 3500 kids in a high school, that leaves out a lot of kids, said Barbara Schneider, a University of Chicago professor and author of "The Ambitious Generation."

How sad I thought, having studied and understood the doctrine of change, that these eminent individuals in our society had such limited comprehension of what leadership was all about.

As the author quite correctly pointed out in the article, the chance of becoming President of the United States occurred only once in every four years or eight years. Based on her analysis of the situation I implied that the odds of her daughter becoming President was a hundred times less than her chance of winning the Power-ball lottery and these were clearly not good odds.

By her analysis I concluded that she was implying that if her daughter was in a smaller class she would have better odds of becoming elected class president and this apparently would propel her towards her dream of one day becoming President of the United States.

She further suggested that a recent 4-H poll of 400 teens said that 90% were more likely to volunteer in their communities after seeing post-September 11 examples of leadership. She then stated that, ***"Though some of the changes needed to nurture this groundswell are already sweeping, such as re-organizing schools to offer more leadership roles, others simply require adults to set aside cynicism and fear, and listen to and support kids' aspirations."***

As I studied this article, I came to some conclusions of my own. My analysis of this article was that the author assumed that the only way a kid could develop into a leader was through practice from being elected to positions in office. This was the point where I disagreed completely with her assumptions. As I have stated previously, **fixed assumptions are self-limiting.**

It appeared to me that the author of the article was suggesting that because her daughter was unlikely to become the President of the United States, that she was likely to go through life, relegated to second-class positions. I concluded that the desire to become president of the United States was because of the presumption that the president wielded great power and she clearly wished that her daughter had the opportunity to wield this power.

I studied the article and wondered why she would not want her daughter to become the Secretary of State instead of the President. Her odds of becoming this would surely be better. Clearly by implication the Secretary of State had less power than the President and so this position was not good enough for our kids.

She clearly could have suggested to her daughter that her odds of becoming Secretary of State were better than that of becoming President and clearly more realistic. Or how about becoming a congressperson or Senator. Again, by implication, these were clearly inferior positions and not good enough for our children.

And how about encouraging her daughter to become a teacher? Is it possible that the author of the article did not feel that this position wielded much power! **Becoming a doctor was clearly out of the question since doctors clearly have no power. What about becoming a lawyer? I guess the cap didn't fit, so she had to (ac)quit that line of thought.**

Poor children of the world! It appears that anyone who could not become the President of the United States was doomed to live a life of servitude. Nevertheless, the author at the end of the article encouraged her daughter to follow her dream with the exhortation, **"You go for it girl!"**

A journalist once asked Mark Twain a question as to whether he felt he (Mark

Twain) was the greatest author in the world. This question was asked at the period when Mark Twain was at the height of his literary prowess.

Twain replied that he did not know who was the greatest author. The journalist then persisted and asked the famous author how he would rate himself compared to other authors; to which Mark Twain replied that he was the second greatest author of all time.

The journalist was flabbergasted and asked Mark Twain how he could be content with the position of second greatest author and why would he not prefer to be recognized as the best of all time. Mark Twain replied that he preferred to be second best because every other author felt that he/she was the best and since there was so much confusion as to who was the best, he preferred the position of second best, since there was absolutely no confusion about that position.

I would not disagree with the mother encouraging her daughter to aspire to becoming the President of the United States **(assuming that the child was born in the USA)**. Clearly to suggest otherwise would be contradictory with my position that you can only be as great as you can dream. But here is another example of where we need to make a paradigm shift.

As for the changes that were sweeping the schools as a consequence of September 11th, I have stated that September 11th forced some changes upon us as a society and **force does not result in meaningful change**. Meaningful change as I have stated repeatedly will only result when we change our mental model. **We must never again wait for a crisis such as September 11th before we recognize the need for change**.

As far as the author's original point regarding leadership and power, it has always been the assumption in most circles that the most powerful person in the world is the President of the United States. Baloney! I disagree!

"Disagree?" you ask. "Certainly!" I reply. "What about Bill Gates?" He controls the computer industry and he is the richest man in the world. Oops! I forgot about Warren Buffet and the Queen of England! No? O.K, then maybe the Chairman of the Federal Reserve, who has the power to cut interest rates or to increase interest rates without the authority of the President. That is real power! With the stroke of a pen he could send stock markets around the world plummeting and the President would have no power to stop him. No? You disagree?

O.K then, how about that Sheik in Saudi Arabia? Isn't he the most powerful man in the world? If they cut off oil supplies to the rest of the world, I am going to freeze to death in this cold Michigan winter **(or maybe I'll just return to sunny Barbados after all). Ah Ha! Maybe it is the Prime Minister of Barbados then. He can refuse me entry into Barbados.**

No, you say? **It seems that we have a major disagreement here.**

So like Mark Twain, I say that *I* will step forward and say that *I* am the **second most powerful person** in the world since no one else wants that position. So there! The problem is now all settled. So why did the author of the Wall Street Journal not encourage her daughter to aspire to my position instead? The answer lies in our mis-perception of what power and leadership is all about.

Frankly, **I think that the most powerful person in the world is a little ten-year-old boy running around with a rock in his hand somewhere in Palestine.**

"You are being a little ridiculous now, aren't you?" You ask. "Absolutely not!" I reply. "Rubbish!" You respond. "Show me your ridiculous line of reasoning!"

"Well", I respond; "Consider that little ten year old with a rock in his hand. The Prime Minister of Israel is in Palestine for a peace meeting with the leader of the Palestine Liberation Organization. As he is getting out of his car, this innocent little boy who has been ignored by the security forces, hurls a rock; which hits the Prime Minister of Israel in his head. The Prime Minister is knocked unconscious and is rushed to the hospital for immediate brain surgery.

The Israelis are madder than hell and launch wave after wave of attacks against the Palestinians. The rest of the Arab world become involved and the United States is dragged into the conflict. The next world war starts, all because of the power of a little ten-year-old boy with a rock in his hand. **"NOW THAT IS POWER!"** I say. Do you concede the argument now? Settled!

The point I wish to make here is that power lies in any individual who has the ability to make a significant difference. Leadership comes from the ability to influence meaningful change in another. We each and every one of us have this ability to make significant differences in us and in others.

Whoever has the ability to effect meaningful change in another has equal power to any other person in the world. Certainly the Present of the United States has the power to launch a nuclear attack against another country but that little ten-year-old boy with a rock in his hand has as much power as any other to start the next world war!

Is there a difference between leadership and power? I suppose that there must be, since the little boy with the rock who has the power to create major problems lacks the ability to have followers as true leaders do. **True leaders then have the ability to influence followers by their ability to effect meaningful change in themselves and others.**

When I started out in the Master of Medical Management program, my aspiration was to become the CEO of my hospital or to become the CEO or COO, (whichever was the more important title) of some large managed care organization; which was ruining my life as a physician.

My reasoning was that I had more ability than all the other 'dummies' **(in my misguided thoughts and through blinkered eyes)** who ran these institutions and of course I could be a better 'dummy'! After my eyes were opened through my understanding of the philosophy, principles and process of change, I realized that I was trying to become the **best** 'dummy' whereas what I **really wanted** was to be recognized as the **second best** 'dummy' (see Mark Twain) **since every one else laid claim to being the best.**

I quickly realized that **a leader is anyone who has the ability to influence meaningful change in others. A leader has vision. A leader is someone who can visualize change before a crisis develops and point others in the right direction.**

A leader is someone who sees what needs to be done and does it or finds someone who can do the job right. A leader does the right thing and shows others how to do the right thing. But most of all, **A LEADER DOES NOT NEED A TITLE.**

In the movie "Saving Private Ryan", starring Tom Hanks, it is the sergeant who has to step forward to lead his men out of trouble after the Captain and Lieutenant are killed. Leaders will emerge through their ideas for effecting meaningful change and will not need titles. **Jesus Christ was the greatest leader of all time but he was never elected to any position. He had more influence than Herod who was the king at that time.**

I no longer aspire to be CEO or CFO or COO or Executive Vice President (as someone recently reminded me of what his proper title was when I referred to him as the Vice President of his company).

But I do want to be a leader and I wish to make leaders of every one who reads this book. I wish to show others how to effect meaningful change in **their** lives and I know that if I can change one single person, then I have the power to change the world.

That makes me a very powerful person and my hope is that **whoever reads this book will become equally powerful**. When we understand that we all have that power to change ourselves and to change others, we can feel better about our role and ourselves in our organizations and our purpose in life.

One of the best examples of a true leader among us is related in the following anecdote:

'In the town of Frankenmuth , Michigan, exists the largest and grandest Christmas store in the world. The name of the store is 'Bronner's' after the owner, Mr. Wally Bronner. This store is open 364 days in the year and specializes in selling only Christmas items. Large Hollywood productions such as the movie 'Santa Claus' usually contract with 'Bronner's to supply them with their props.

Wally Bronner has held court with virtually every President in recent times and there are pictures on the walls of the store with Mr. and Mrs. Bronner in the presence of Presidents and other celebrities.

There is an Urgent Care facility in Frankenmuth to which Mr. Bronner donated a plaque with the poem 'Footprints in the Sand.' One day, Mr.Bronner came to the Urgent Care facility for minor care. We noticed that he was looking at the plaque. After he had left, someone noticed that the plaque was missing. No one knew who had taken the plaque. About two weeks later, the plaque reappeared on the wall, in a new frame.

Apparently Mr. Bronner had noticed that the plaque had been damaged and took it upon himself to repair it and did so without any fanfare. This act epitomizes what a true leader is all about. Mr. Bronner is a pillar and a leader in his community. He looks for what needs to be done and he does it.'

Apathy in organizations arises when individuals feel that they have no power to effect meaningful change. Those individuals feel that the only people with the power to make a difference are the people with the titles and since they have little or no chance in the hierarchy of the system to become the "Chief", then their contribution in the organization is not valued. **Empowerment is when we recognize that we all have equal power as the next person and we do not ask for permission to do the right thing. We just do it, just like Mr. Bronner and every other great leader.**

I hope that the ten-year-old girl at the beginning of this chapter becomes President one day. But if she doesn't, I hope that she becomes a true leader and realizes that she would have as much power as the President to make a difference.

As for the rest of you out there who do not wish to be President, there is nothing wrong with being second-best. Ask Mark Twain.

So go out there and lead the rest of the world through change!

CHAPTER 15

Our World And The Need For Change

When we let freedom ring, when we let it ring from every village and every hamlet, from every state and every city, we will be able to speed up that day when all of God's children, black men and white men, Jews and Gentiles, Protestants and Catholics, will be able to join hands and sing in the words of the old Negro spiritual, "Free at last! Free at last! Thank God almighty we are free at last"
Martin Luther King Jr.
'I have a dream'

O Little Town of Bethlehem, How (Still?) We See Thee Lie.

I look at the problems facing our world today and my heart is filled with sadness and disappointment and I remain amazed that we **choose** to live our lives in abject misery and **constant conflict. But I am full of enthusiasm and hope that through understanding the concept of effecting meaningful change, we can make the world, as we would like it to be, for us and for the generations that will follow us.**

This week (as I write this book) a dozen Israelis were killed in an explosion in Tel Aviv. Last week Israeli rockets in Palestine killed five Palestinian children. Troops are lined up at the border between India and Pakistan, ready to launch nuclear rockets designed to annihilate each other.

These depressing news are repeated week in and week out. Dozens of Palestinian suicide bombers have killed themselves and others by exploding bombs in Israel. In return, the Israelis have rained rocket attacks on Palestine killing numerous Palestinians.

The Prime Minister of Israel points his finger at the leader of the Palestine Liberation Organization and the PLO leader points his finger right back at the Israeli leader.

Each side continues to blame each other and neither side is willing to accept any element of responsibility for the ongoing problem. Neither side is willing to seriously examine the other side's arguments and to see where they could compromise. Neither side could see that if they were to work together that they would each benefit greatly and **NO ONE NEEDS TO LOSE ANYTHING**.

Israelis it would appear prefer living with their gas masks and austere security laws and Palestinians it would appear seem content to live in their refugee camps hurling rocks at Israeli tanks and planes. **Or so it would seem**. Why else would neither side make a genuine and concerted attempt to solve their problems?

The answer clearly lies in each side being **unwilling to change,** or being **unable to see** how to effect meaningful change that would be acceptable to the other side and result in each party being able to live, as they would really like to do.

Do people really prefer to live in conflict and misery as they do or are they simply unable to see alternative, better solutions?

I suggest that it is the **inability to effect meaningful change in us and our inability to understand how to effect meaningful change in others** is what lies at the root of all of our problems.

People need to learn and understand the "Process of Change". This is no less applicable to our political leaders as it is to individuals, business corporations, and organizations and in personal relationships.

In the Middle East, it would seem that some of the politicians and the vocal minority who resist change want to live in the past. These individuals' values and culture seems not to have evolved over two thousand years of civilization.

In keeping with the postulate that lack of change will result in decline and decay and ultimately death, my prediction then is that unless the parties seek meaningful change, they will underwrite their own self-destruction. **But it is never too late for change** to occur and **hopefully someone from the Middle East will read this book.**

If we look around the world today we can see so much need for meaningful change, **real** change. **It is the responsibility of each and every one of us to examine every aspect of our lives and to take an active role in effecting the necessary changes.**

In an earlier section of this book, I stated that if you threw a pebble in a pond, the ripples would spread all around the globe and the energy from those ripples would eventually come right back to its source.

In Chicago, there is a group, 'The Chicago Symphony Orchestra' that creates beautiful music. This group is led by the conductor Daniel Barenbom, an Argentinean Jew and consists of young musicians from Egypt, Lebanon, Israel and other middle-eastern countries, working together to create beautiful music.

Two of these musicians are Saleem Aboud Ashkar, an Egyptian and Shai Wosner, an Israeli Jew and I had the opportunity to hear them perform a fantastic piano duet together. The following are words from these two fine musicians working together to create beautiful music that neither one could have achieved, performing solo:

"When you are born within war, it is difficult to see how things could be different,' says Saleem Ashkar, the Egyptian.

"Our performance together is hopefully a preview into the future about what we could achieve together. It is an opportunity for others to see what beautiful music we could create together," says Shai Wosner, the Jew.

When the tragedy of September 11th occurred there were people around the globe who cheered. These people felt that America had been dealt a major blow. They were correct in this assumption but where they were mistaken was in the assumption that they themselves were immune from the effects of that despicable action. How wrong they were!

The effect of the major crisis as occurred on September 11th was to show the world how inter-connected we all are. On that black day in September, the rest of the world stood still. International airline traffic was brought to a standstill. International business transactions ceased. Billions of dollars were lost by every nation on this earth.

The tourism trade around the globe experienced a downturn. Small countries like Jamaica and Barbados; which rely on tourism as the mainstay of their economy will feel the effects of September 11th for years to come.

The huckster who relies on making a living from selling handmade jewelry on the beach will feel the effects of the downturn in the economy just as acutely as the CEO of Cantor Fitzgerald who lost seven hundred of his employees and friends and family in the disaster.

Switzerland, which claims neutrality in international affairs, suffered as greatly as any other nation when tourism experienced a downturn. Swissair, the national airline of Switzerland filed for bankruptcy. This further affected the national economy. When President Bush put a block on terrorist funds, this put further pressure on the Swiss economy. **So much for being neutral!** Even my brother and his family who travel frequently to Florida with Swissair had to cut back on their vacations.

Travel to Mecca in Saudi Arabia was severely restricted, depriving millions of Muslims from around the world from making their holy pilgrimage; which is such an important aspect of every Muslim's life. Remember that the action of the terrorists was allegedly to promote the cause of Islam. Of course the economy of Saudi Arabia also suffered.

And what about the terrorists themselves? Well, just like the rock in the water whose ripples come right back to the source, the terrorists were revisited by their own ripples in a manner that they never imagined. Today the terrorist organization in Afghanistan has been eradicated. The Taliban Government in Afghanistan is no more.

So who suffered in the aftermath of September 11th? **We all did**. Muslims, Jews, Christians, Buddhists, Hindus, Scientologists all suffered in equal manner. **This was never a purely United States tragedy. This was a tragedy of the world. This was**

159

a tragedy of humanity.

A crisis of major proportions was required for us to realize how inter-connected we all are. If a fire had occurred in Chicago and destroyed an apartment complex and only ten people were killed, the people in Brazil or Peru would not blink an eye.

We required a crisis as major and as shocking as September 11th to jolt us all and awaken our senses. **Even Osama Bin Laden could not imagine the extent of the devastation that his agents could cause and even he could not imagine the wrath that would rain on him!**

We must recognize that meaningful change is possible in all of us and we all have the capacity to make meaningful change in others. We need to acquire the tools and learn the process of change to lead more fulfilling lives. If you question the purpose of another book like this, then answer me as to why we have problems such as we have in the world today!

We must recognize that force and violence do not result in meaningful change. I cannot emphasize this point often enough. Both the Arabs and the Israelis have used force to attempt to convince each other to change. Neither side has succeeded so far and neither side will, as long as they continue to employ these techniques.

Meaningful change will only result when Israelis and Palestinians decide to change their mental model.

'When I lived in Glasgow, Scotland as a young student at Glasgow University, I had as a roommate a young Jewish student named Ehud Libis. For one week, Ehud would not speak to me and whenever I entered the room, Ehud would turn his back to me and face the wall. This unpleasant state of affairs went on for a whole week until I could stand it no more. I decided to ask for a change of roommate but before I did so, I mentioned the problem to a Scottish friend named Michael Inglis.

Michael approached Ehud to find out what was the problem since according to him, Ehud was a nice guy. The problem as it turned out was that Ehud assumed that I was an Arab because of my appearance. When he discovered that I was not in fact an Arab, his attitude changed and we became the best of friends. Ehud was a very well off student financially, unlike me who was getting by on a shoestring budget.

One day, I took him to an Indian restaurant and introduced him to Indian foods such as curries and I paid for the treat. He in turn later introduced me to all his Jewish friends and I became familiar with the Jewish community in Glasgow and I learnt about and enjoyed Jewish foods.

After I introduced Ehud to Indian curry, he became such a fan of this type of food, he wanted me to take him to the Indian restaurants every day and <u>he volunteered to pay for both of our meals</u>. Every time we went to the restaurant he would say in his strong Jewish accent, "No, no Andrew! My turn, my turn! (So much for the ridicu-

lous stereotype of Jews being cheap.)

Of course I never objected too strongly to his offers. I guess one reason I never objected too strongly was because Ehud had done his national service in the Israeli navy. **But I think that the bigger reason was because I didn't object to getting some free meals.**

Nevertheless we both became winners. He learnt about and enjoyed delicious Indian curry dishes and <u>I was the beneficiary of many free meals</u>, which, if you have ever been a struggling college student is always appreciated. *To be honest, I thought that I was the bigger winner, but Ehud didn't seem to mind. And who was I to complain.'*

I lost touch with Ehud after I left Scotland but I have fond memories of our relation to this day. I developed a better understanding of Jewish people and he learnt that you should not judge others by their external appearance and I know that we were both richer for our experience.

I hope that Ehud is one of those people in Israel today who is using the experience we both gained from our relationship to try to effect meaningful change in the relationship between Israel and Palestine.

If only someone could show the Israelis and Palestinians the tremendous economic benefits to change. I theorize that Israel and Palestine have the potential to become the wealthiest countries in the world, if only they could agree to peaceful co-existence.

Both countries could accumulate vast wealth simply from selling dirt in bottles. Billions of tourists would flock to Jerusalem to visit the Holy Land. Billions of tourists would willingly part with their money just to say that they were in possession of dirt from the holy land.

Disney world would pale in comparison to Jerusalem and Bethlehem. People would flock just to see the big rock that was placed in front of Jesus' tomb. No maintenance would be required. No electricity would be required to run the place. The only person required would be a gatekeeper to collect the huge sums of money that willing tourists would dump at their feet. Neither country would have enough hotel rooms to accommodate the hordes of tourists.

The same situation applies to Egypt, Syria, Iraq, Iran and Saudi Arabia. These countries wouldn't need to sell another drop of oil. They could afford to give away their oil dirt-cheap. But I am dreaming, am I not? Actually I am very serious!

The same problems face the people of Northern Ireland and North Korea, Cuba, India and Pakistan, Indonesia and Nigeria, Sri Lanka and the Philippines and **even the good** old USA.

In the USA (like so many other countries of the world), we face the problems of racism, bigotry, intolerance of diversity and discrimination. We see inner city projects ignored by both Governmental agencies and private agencies, because 'their problems are not our problems'. Really?

Do we seriously believe that the inner city problems will not come up to haunt us some day? Remember that every ripple spreads around the world and the ripples that we create will come right back to us. **Ask Osama Bin Laden the truth of this theory?**

If we do not seek to effect meaningful change to address the <u>world's</u> problems, we have no one else but us to blame for the decline and decay that will follow. Racism and discrimination are as much **our** problem as our Aunt Gertie having to have surgery for cancer of her colon.

Starvation and hunger in Africa are as much a part of our problem as the credit card bills that we must pay each month. Giving cups of rice or wheat to feed the starving in Africa is not meaningful change. **Teaching them how to effect meaningful change and helping them to do so is.**

When some stranger in New York City loses her job because of the September 11th tragedy, it is as much a problem for us as when our own brother loses his job.

When some child in Afghanistan or Russia suffers from the cold of their bitter winter and the pangs of hunger from their empty stomachs, it is as much a part of our problem as when we cannot find that extra quarter to super-size our fries.

When thirty five million people remain without medical insurance in the United States, it is as much of a problem **for us** as it is a problem for us when individuals in Africa or China cannot afford medication to treat their AIDS **and it is a problem for all of us**.

If we think otherwise, the problems that will visit us are like nothing that we can ever imagine.

And the only way that we will find effective solutions to these problems is to learn how to effect meaningful change in us and to teach others how to make meaningful change!

CHAPTER 16

The "Magical" Mirror Experiment

> **We Each Have the Power to Choose**
> *The wind changes directions a hundred times or more a day. It has no goal or focus to be anything more than itself. The wind is free to come and go as it pleases. But people, on the other hand, have an inner desire to accomplish, to achieve, and to be productive. It is a human quality that enables people to select which way they want to go and to determine how fast or how slow their journey will be. People have the power to choose the roads they will travel. They must never forget that they are in control of their lives.*
> **Deanna Beisser**
> **"Is it time to change?"**

What exactly is the magical mirror experiment and exactly how does it work? The mirror experiment as I employ it in my teaching of the process of change is key to getting people to understanding the six fundamental steps in the process of change. Whenever I stand a subject in front of the mirror, I tell them that my mirror is a magical mirror.

It never fails to amaze me that no matter what the social or professional status of my subjects who are seeking change; whenever I tell them that I have a special magical mirror they always seem to believe. As I have developed the technique, I am similarly convinced of the 'magical' properties of the mirror when I see the dramatic responses after I conduct my experiment.

When I conduct the "mirror-experiment" I advise the subject(s) that my mirror will reveal things that they never believed could be possible. I tell them that my mirror will make them into whatever **they** want to be and that **my mirror can change people in ways they never believed possible**. "This is why," I tell them, "my mirror is magical." In truth, this is exactly what happens by the time I have finished conducting the test and the subjects actually come to see that what I have been telling them are true.

I am yet to see a single person who hasn't experienced positive change after I have conducted my experiment. I have seen tears come into the eyes of macho men and tough young men after I have finished my experiment. The quizzical looks that I get from the subjects sometimes leave me with the feeling that there is something magical in the mirror. The look I usually get is one of, "What the heck did you just do with me?"

The youngest person that I have changed through use of the mirror-experiment was eight years old and I have actually got a 'non-compliant' physician to see the need for change through using the mirror.

There are many variations as to how this experiment can be conducted but like everything else mastery of the process only comes through repeated practice and each of us will develop our individualized styles.

In teaching others how to conduct the mirror experiment, I first invite the subject(s) requesting or needing change to stand in front of a mirror and I then take them through the process in a very deliberate and calm and organized manner.

<u>Step 1</u>. Recognizing the need for change.
Stand in front of the mirror and observe and picture everything about yourself, both good and bad and see if change is needed and possible.

I first invite them to **observe their image in the mirror and to see themselves as they are in the present**. They are invited to picture everything about themselves in totality and to see everything, both good and bad about themselves. I may ask them to express in their own words what they see in the mirror or to simply hold the image in their mind.

<u>Step 2</u>. Visualize the future.
Project an image of yourself at a selected point in time in the future, as you would **like** to see yourself.

This is probably the most important link in the chain of the process of change. This is where individuals see the opportunity to invent their own future and if they are sincere about making meaningful change this is the step that will influence their decision. This is where they see the **benefits to change** and they also are made to see the **consequences of no change**.

They are able to see themselves as **they** would like to be and this is when the mirror reveals it's magical properties.

I invite them to look over their **right** shoulder and to select any point in time **in the future** and to project the image of them, as **they** would like to see themselves **at that point in time**. I invite them to take a long hard look at that image of how **they** would like to be or how they would like to feel or how they would like to be in their relationship or in their career or business.

The mirror experiment helps the subject(s) to develop a realistic image of them and to see goals that are realistic, since the image that **they** project is what **they** create and not what someone else has created for them.

I also always insist that they look over their **left** shoulder and picture an image of them **if they make no change**. The dejected look that comes across their faces when they see that image is usually enough to clinch the deal. **I am yet to meet anyone who preferred the image on the left**. As I have stated in a previous chapter, my choice of the right shoulder for the positive image and the left shoulder for the negative image is no mere coincidence.

It reinforces in their psyche that **right side** represents the **right choices** and the **left side** represents **what is left** if they make no change.

Many individuals are brought to tears at this point. The line of questioning may go something like this: "So tell me Jack, do you like what you see? Can you see yourself getting to where you want to be? How do you think you will get there? If they have not already asked for the tissues, they will probably ask for them now.

If by this time the subject hasn't seen the need for change, you could pack your bags and go on to another subject. I haven't seen a single person who has not committed to change when I use the mirror technique.

<u>Step 3</u>. Accept the need for chaange.
Decide whether you are satisfied with the image in the mirror or whether you would like to see things changed for the better.

Whether or not the subject is satisfied with the image in the mirror, I will usually ask the subject(s) whether they see any need for change or whether it is possible that they can improve the image with any type of change. This gets them to accept the need for change.

It is crucial to understand that in the mirror experiment, as I practice it, that **it is not always necessary for the subject to be dissatisfied with the image in the mirror**. The principal purpose of the mirror experiment is for the subject to **recognize the need for change and to accept that things need to be different and to recognize that there is always room for improvement.**

For example, if we are dealing with couples, one of the parties might be comfortable with their present circumstance and might not recognize the necessity for change. If such individuals are content with their present status then I ask if they can see opportunities for improvement in the relationship.

On the other hand the majority of subjects will express the fact that they do not like their present image. **"Isn't this why they are consulting you in the first place?"**

Step 4. Desire for change.
The subject (s) must want to change and say this openly.

At this point, the individual(s) must **want** to experience change and they usually do. The problem is that at this point the subject is confused as to how to go about achieving the **objective of effecting meaningful change. This is where guidance becomes necessary**. If the subject(s) are still undecided about the possibility of meaningful change or are unsure of the need, I may skip this step and move on to the next step in the process and then return to this step.

I must emphasize that it is not necessary to be rigid in following the exact sequence of steps and it is possible to start from any point and work around from that point. As you master the technique, you will develop your own style of conducting the exercise.

Step 5. Plan for change.
Develop a mental map to take you into the future.

To illustrate the concept of the mental map, I find it helpful to use the analogy of the subject taking a long trip by car to some exotic destination. I might ask them to picture them taking a trip to some nice place, starting from their present location. I point out to them that they will be driving themselves or if someone else is driving, then **their** responsibility is to be the navigator.

The concept of them driving themselves by car is important since it emphasizes to them that **they** are **in control** of their journey and **they cannot rely on someone else taking them to their destination as for instance if they were going by plane.**

I remind them of the journey that they are about to embark on and invite them to tell me how they anticipate getting to their ultimate destination or the image of themselves as they have projected in the future. I remind them that in order to get from where they currently are to the point where they want to be, they must use a map. I point out to them that like any map, the directions are usually clear about which route to follow. Veering off their route could result in them losing their way. I emphasize the point that they need to be consistent in following the route they have planned.

Step 6. Implementing the plan.
Embarking on your journey of following your mental map to your destination.

The subject(s) are then invited to visualize their mental map as they are about to embark on their destination into the future that they have invented for them. I remind them that in any long journey, that there may be intersections and diversions where the signs may be confusing to them. In these circumstances they need a local guide and I point out that my role is to be the guide.

This is when they, like all of us will need directions from locals to point them in the right direction. Or, as in any type of long journey, they will occasionally need to have their gas tanks refilled. I point out to them that my role as a consultant or physician is to act as the local guide, pointing them back onto the highway or like the gas station owner; I am there to refill their gas tanks with gasoline (medicine when needed). **My clients are usually amused when I tell them that I am only a gas station attendant or local guide along the highway to their destination**

The mirror experiment helps the subject(s) to develop a realistic image of them and to set goals that are realistic, since the image that they project is what they create and not what someone else has created for them.

My objective is to create a **"can do"** image rather than the previously held negative images or the apathetic feelings that so many of them usually might hold of the future when they first come to me.

The following is an example of how the actual mirror experiment is conducted:

By the time I get to Phoenix she'll be dreaming.

Sometimes the responses can be downright funny. Gabrielle M (a pseudonym) was a patient who came to see me after several other doctors had rejected her from their practices. She suffered with chronic pain and was on several types of pain medication. She walked with a cane even though she was only thirty-five years old. **Clearly she had genuine pain**. Why else would a thirty-five year old attractive young lady choose to walk with a cane and with a genuinely pronounced limp? **(Even when no one appeared to be looking)**.

But the last doctor and several doctors before that she had seen, had labeled her as a drug-seeker and they were only too happy to discharge her to my care. She was also severely asthmatic and had serious environmental allergies. She had been a smoker until recently. She quit temporarily after she had been admitted to the hospital with pneumonia and respiratory failure and had been placed on a ventilator.

Gabrielle M came to my practice seeking help to quit smoking permanently because her near death experience with respiratory failure and the fact that she had needed to be placed on a ventilator to help her breathing. As a result she desperately wanted to quit smoking but she was not certain if she could succeed on her own without using some type of smoking aid such as one of the pills that was available for help with smoking cessation. She had previously used these pills on two occasions **(without success I might add)**. Her statement when she came to me was, "Doc, I would like to try the new drug. It's called Welbutrin. I think it's the generic form of Zyban".

The truth was that **Zyban is the alternative name for Welbutrin, an anti-depressant drug that had been on the market for years. The manufacturer simply changed the name and the packaging and with the blessing of the FDA convinced the public that a new drug had been discovered that would miraculously get people to quit smoking!**

The FDA actually bought into what to me is a gimmick and approved this drug with a change of its new name for smoking cessation! I am yet to see any significant difference, in my own practice, in the success rate achieved through using this drug versus using nothing at all.

In fact, since using my new technique for dealing with smoking cessation, I have achieved far superior results at less cost compared to using expensive drugs with their attendant side effects. And I am convinced that the results I have achieved

with my techniques will be more meaningful and longer lasting.

The new trend in the pharmaceutical industry is to assign different names to old drugs with claims for newer indications when the patent life on the old drugs is about to expire. This is a deplorable trend and results in no meaningful improvements in healthcare.

But the FDA, which apparently has bought into the claims of the pharmaceutical industry, supports the trend. If only physicians could get their patients to buy in to their recommendations as easily as the FDA buys in to the pharmaceutical industry claims regarding these 'new drugs.' All of our problems in healthcare would disappear overnight.

I still have acres of beachfront property in Arizona and I think I will target as potential customers the people who run the FDA.

I can only suppose that the FDA agrees to the name changes for these drugs because they see no alternative ways for dealing with issues of major public health concern such as getting people to quit smoking and like the drowning man, they are clutching at straws!

In the case of my patient Gabrielle, she wanted help controlling her pain, which had developed following a previous car accident from many years past. She clearly wanted help to turn her life around and I was convinced of the genuiness of her requests and I really wanted to help her.

She also specifically expressed her concern about how some of her past narcotic pain medications had made her unable to function well and she requested something that would help her to control her pain and yet be able to resume her studies at the local university.

Gabrielle also explained to me that she really did not like how some of the narcotic pain medications made her feel and although she needed to have her pain treated, she really would prefer something that did not make her dopey.

She confessed to me that she had once been a user of marijuana and cocaine and had been clean for over one year and really did not want medication that would rekindle her previous addictive behavior. She explained to me that she really wanted to turn her life around and proclaimed with joy and excitement that she had a planned trip to Florida where she had relatives residing.

In my discussion with Gabrielle, I recognized that she had a wonderful and funny personality and sense of humor and my heart warmed to her. Here was a wonderful person who because of her past behaviors was being abandoned by people who were supposed to be committed to caring for others.

This was a wonderful person who had seen psychologists and psychiatrists, seeking help and knew the names of all the anti-depressant medications by heart but had never obtained the real help that she needed; **which was to learn how to make meaningful changes in her life**.

I didn't feel as much sadness for Gabrielle as I felt for the professionals who had treated her in the past. **It was at times like this when I realized that if people really understood how to effect meaningful change in others, then there would be no need for a book such as this.**

It was clear to me that this was a person who genuinely wanted help, who was genuinely in pain and who genuinely wanted to turn her life around but had never been offered meaningful help for change.

My heart went out to this poor unfortunate woman who through the circumstances of her environment had made some poor decisions in the past and was now expected to suffer for the rest of her life. I recognized her genuine desire to change and I desperately wanted to help her change. I proceeded to take her through the mirror experiment as follows:

I took Gabrielle through the mirror experiment as I have described in other sections of this book, in the following manner.

I first asked Gabrielle M to stand in front of the mirror and to visualize the image that she saw in the mirror. I then asked her how she felt about the image that she saw in the mirror and whether she liked the image. She grimaced, frowned and answered, " No, I do not like it one bit!" This by the way was a fairly attractive young lady physically. But the image she saw was not of a physically beautiful person but that of someone who had made a mess of her life.

I then asked Gabrielle if she would like to be able to change the image that she saw in the mirror. Her answer was, "Definitely!"

I next asked her to look over her **right** shoulder and to visualize an image of how she would like to see herself ten years into the future. She pondered, looked and a glimmer of a smile appeared on her face. A beam of light appeared in her eyes and she firmly answered, "O.K, I got it!" I asked her if she liked what she saw but I knew the answer even before I had asked the question.

I then asked this poor unfortunate soul how she expected to get to the image of herself as she saw the image in the mirror. She answered that she was not sure.

At this point, I usually have to help the subject(s) understand what I am trying to get them to think by introducing an analogy of a trip that they might plan to some far distant place. In this instance, I asked Gabrielle to imagine that she was going on a trip to somewhere far away that she liked.

170

Another smile broke out on her face and when I asked her where she might want to go, she replied, "Phoenix, Arizona." I mentioned that Phoenix was indeed a desirable destination and a beautiful city since I had just recently visited there and I asked her how she would expect to get there. She said, "I'll fly of course!" This was clearly not the answer I expected and so I suggested to her that since we were just experiencing the tragedy of September 11th, that she might consider driving. She said that was also fine by her since she had done so before.

I then asked her since she was going to Phoenix, what type of preparation she was going to make to get there. Her answer was, "I'll get my hair done and get some new clothes." This still was not the answer I wanted; so I subtly suggested that she might also want to get a map and plan her trip since Phoenix was so far away. She promptly replied, **"NOT for Phoenix Doc! I've been there too often! I don't need a map for Phoenix! I can get to Phoenix blindfolded"**

I was stumped for words and the only response I could elicit was that since it was summertime that there were likely to be a lot of orange cones from road construction and maybe a lot of traffic diversions and so she really should have a map. After she insisted that she knew too well how to get to Phoenix, I suggested that she might want to plan a trip to Stinking Creek Road in Tennessee, a place where she had never been. She laughed but I reassured her that Stinking Creek Road was really a nice place. **(There really is such a place in Tennessee).**

The point is that I try to get the subject to understand that in the same way that they would expect to use a map to get to a physical destination, so too would they need a map to get to the mental image that they have projected for their future. This exercise is all about **inventing your own future**. After all as I tell the subject(s), **if you do not invent your own future, someone else is likely to invent your future and it might not be what you like.**

The next step in the process is to ask them how they would expect to fare if they **did not** use the map to get to their ultimate destination. The idea is for them to realize that if they did not have a predetermined destination, that they could likely end up in some remote God-forsaken and desolate place quite unlike where they intended to be.

Such a destination might be fraught with danger, bandits and ugly scenery. Similarly if they did not have a map, they are just as likely to get lost even though they knew their predetermined destination.

If the subject(s) have difficulty expressing the fact that they need to make the meaningful change to get them to their ultimate destination, I will re-emphasize this fact to them. Very few people however fail to recognize and express this fact. This is because the mirror opens people's eyes

The transformation is usually complete by this point. Sometimes they look at me in shock and horror. If by this time they have not got the message that change is needed, chances are that they never will. By this time, they have firmly resolved that major changes are necessary to take them to their preconceived destination.

Many a smoker has quit cold turkey right at this point. **Gabrielle left my office deciding that she no longer wanted or needed any pills to help her quit smoking. She decided there and then that she was quitting permanently and that she did not need any type of pills to help her.**

I did prescribe some non-narcotic medication for her pain and she was extremely happy. She left my office with grateful thanks and a changed person. The last time I saw her, she had still quit smoking and I feel confident that her decision to quit is permanent.

This then is the basis of the Mirror Experiment as **I** employ it and as **I** have designed it. When I choose to have the subject(s) visualize the **positive image** on the **right** side and the **negative image** on the **left** side, it is no mere coincidence. I emphasize that the positive image is on the right because that is what they will experience when they make the **right changes**. The negative image on the left is what is left if they make no meaningful change. As one subject said, "The image on the left is **LOSER Doc. L is for loser.** "

Anyone can learn this technique and anyone can be taught this very simple technique. **Mastery requires constant practice.**

Learn it well, practice it repeatedly and soar off into the future! Change someone else.

Man in the mirror
Michael Jackson

CHAPTER 17

Conclusion

When I conceived this book, I desired to employ the philosophy of change as **I** had conceptualized it **in my own way** and I hoped that my approach to the subject would be different from others who have preceded me in dealing with this subject.

In this way I hoped that the contents of my book would in itself fulfill the objectives implicit in its title, which is, **"How to effect meaningful change."** That is why I have elected to develop **my own** philosophy and promoted my own concept of the process of **change in a simple manner** so that everyone reading this book could implement the process in his/her life or organization.

I have simplified the process of change to **six simple steps** to make it easy for anyone to understand and to be able to follow the process. I believe that this in itself is meaningful change and differs significantly from what others have recommended in the past.

I believe that the process as described in this book is quite different from what others have previously described and what is currently out there. **If it were not, then this book would probably be irrelevant.** I have described in this book the same type of philosophy and process that I have employed in **my** clinical practice, with visible success in virtually every aspect of my patients' healthcare.

As I have stated previously and repeatedly, these same principles are applicable whether they are used by individuals or in personal relationships or in the broader context of organizations or your community or in developing your spirituality.

Had I not seen the success of my techniques reflected in my patients' improvement and well-being and in my own life and practice, **I would have been better off spending my evenings at the golf dome practicing my golf swing while waiting for Spring to come around and saved myself all the money that my 'friends' will inevitably take from me on the golf course.**

If my patients had not demonstrated improvements from their lifestyle changes, through employing the principles and process of change as described in this book, I could have spent my time more usefully trying to predict the direction the stock market would take and try to pick which stocks would be good investments.

But I choose to invest my time in the development of my fellow man because I believe that the returns will be greater in terms of my contribution to society and

the returns from society will be greater when we see the results of meaningful change.

If the patients who benefited from the principles and process of change as I taught them had not **insisted** that I write this book and **pleaded** that I get it out quickly, I would have been better off taking that long awaited vacation to sunny Barbados that I have deferred for some time now.

The benefits, as I have seen in just the improvement in my patients' lives, is in itself justification for a book such as this.

This book is not intended for **me** to provide solutions to **your problems. That would be defeating the principle of meaningful change. The objective is to guide people to find <u>their own</u> solutions to their <u>own unique set of problems</u>. The objective of the book is to show why we need to seek out meaningful change and how to go about the process.**

The concept of **inter-connectedness** is profound and underlies my feeling of **my own obligation** to share my thoughts with as many people as I can. **I believe that all of us who learn the process of change have the same obligation to teach others to do the same.**

Through my study and understanding of the process, I realized that the same principles and process of "how to effect meaningful change" are as applicable to individuals and their healthcare as they are to personal relationships, careers, businesses, organizations, our world and our spiritual being; and **that makes this book relevant to everyone in our society.**

I have tried to simplify the principles and processes described in this book so that they are as easily understandable and practical to follow by the man in the street, as they would be to members of the Mensa Society. The process has been broken down into six simple steps that are easy for anyone to follow and for anyone wishing to teach others how to do so.

The need for learning how to effect meaningful change is as applicable to the combatants in the Middle East as it is to the teachers in the classroom trying to improve behaviors in their ADHD students and equally as applicable to the auto-industry and the technology companies trying to promote growth in these companies.

Sporting organizations will also benefit from learning and utilizing the processes described in this book. **Is it asking too much to hope that the Detroit Lions football team can use the principles in this book and make it to the next Super Bowl?**

I have taken tools that are used in business, economics, philosophy, and marketing and negotiation and conflict resolution and utilized these tools to refine and shape the principles of change as I have described in this book.

I have consciously avoided replicating studies by other authors as far as their principles because I wanted this book to reflect <u>my own thoughts and philosophy</u>, since I believe that this is the only way that I could achieve my objectives in writing this book, which is to make a significant difference in how others approach life.

It is true that there are many other books with similar intent as this; so it is fair to question the need for another book such as this and ask the question, **"Why?"** but I look around me and see our failures of the past and the present and I respond by asking the question **"Why not?"**

Although other books have similar **intent**, I seriously doubt that any other book contains similar **content**. **I also hope that my style is different from others so that the maximum number of people will benefit from reading the book.**

I understand and accept that I will not reach everyone out there who needs to make meaningful change in his/her lives. Reality tells me that this book is simply another resource in the vast armamentarium out there to help others make those meaningful changes in their lives that will allow them to maximize their potential and to keep them growing physically, mentally and spiritually.

My understanding of the philosophy of change teaches me that **whether I succeed in changing one person or a thousand, that the ripple effect can spread around the world**. And believe me, with the present state of affairs in the world, we do need a lot of change, meaningful ones that is.

If you think that you already have an understanding of the philosophy of change, then I hope that some of the stories in the book will inspire and motivate you to greater heights. As Tiger Woods, the consummate golfer has stated, **"There's always room for improvement.**

This book was developed out of a genuine love and concern for humanity. My own understanding of the need for meaningful change in our lives has renewed and reinvigorated my own spirituality and made a major change **in my life**. I hope it will do the same for each and every one of you who takes the time to read this book.

I have shown through the use of diagrams and the use of real-life examples the reality that for growth and development, change **must** occur. **The question then is no longer whether change is necessary or even whether it is time to change as Deanna Beisser asks in her beautifully written inspirational book. The burning question is, "Why would anyone, having seen all the benefits from change, not want to change?** The question should not be, "Is it time to change?" but rather it should be, **"How and how soon can we change?"**

My fervent hope is that this book will help to teach others why and how to make **meaningful** change and show how we can help others to recognize the need to do the same. In this way, everyone can have the opportunity to enjoy the beauty that this life has to offer us.

Read and study the principles in this book and read it over and over again. And go out there with a renewed outlook on life and CHANGE AND TEACH OTHERS HOW TO CHANGE! Good luck!

> **Change is not a one time process.**
> **Change must be ongoing for it**
> **to be meaningful.**

Figure 9

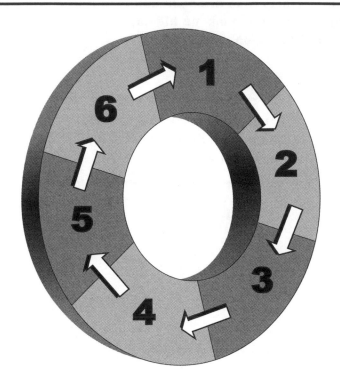

The Wheel of Change

1. Recognize need to change.
2. Visualize positive change/ or consequence of no change.
3. Accept need to change.
4. Desire change.
5. Plan map for change.
6. Implement plan for change.